50
COMPLETE GOALKEEPING TRAINING SESSIONS

Tamara Browder Hageage

Throughout this book, the masculine shall be deemed to include the feminine and vice versa.

ISBN -10: 1-58518-994-4
ISBN -13: 1-58518-994-6
Library of Congress Control Number: 2006932534
Book layout and diagrams: Deborah Oldenburg
Cover design: Studio J Art & Design
Text photos: Tamara Browder Hageage
Front cover photo: Tamara Browder Hageage
Back cover photo: Bente Skjoldager

Coaches Choice
P.O. Box 1828
Monterey, CA 93942
www.coacheschoice.com

Dedication

This book is dedicated to my little number one—my son, George.

George John Hageage IV
21 months old

Acknowledgments

The older I get, the more I believe that the greatest gift the game of soccer gives me is the many wonderful people that I get to meet. Every time I sat down to work on this book, I was reminded of how lucky I am to work in this profession. First, I would like to thank my family. Although you all live hundreds of miles away, I think about you all the time and I have the phone bill to prove it. Thank you to my husband, George, for his constant love and support. You make my life complete. To my son, George, a super-special thank you for taking long afternoon naps giving me time to write this book. You are my sunshine.

Thank you, Amy Griffin—U.S National Team player, World Cup champion, feature commentator for the ESPN, NBC, and Fox networks, USSF "A" coaching license, current assistant coach and goalkeeper coach for the University of Washington, super soccer mom, and I could go on and on. I am extremely honored to have you write the foreword. As a player, I envied and admired you, and after working with you as a coach, I envy and admire you!

I would like to thank Angie Taylor and Coach Darin Lovat for their contributions and professional expertise. Having worked with both of them the past four years, I knew their words could only make my book better.

A very special thank you to Caitlin Braun, Tiera Como, Brandon Johnson, Ryan Johnson, Eric Kurimura, Kali Paris, and Kim Robinson for posing for the photos in this book. You are all awesome players and people. I would also like to thank Eastern Washington University and the Spokane Valley Junior Soccer Association for allowing me to use their facilities for the photo shoot.

I am very grateful to Coach Lesle Gallimore. Although she may not believe me, she had a huge impact on my college career. Inviting me out to participate in the spring of my senior year—when she was first hired—trumped even graduation that June. She has done nothing but tremendous things for the women's program at the University of Washington. Your support means so much. Thank you. To my dear friend, Coach John Leaney, a heartfelt thank you. Anyone who is lucky enough to know John loves him. Considering he is the head men's and women's coach of both of the nationally ranked soccer programs at Macalester College, not to mention a new father to one beautiful boy named Jack, I *really* appreciate you taking the time to endorse my book. You're still the best. I am also very grateful to Coach Randy Waldrum, whom I had the pleasure to meet in the summer of 2004 (yes, just before he lead Notre Dame to victory in the

NCAA Division I National Championship) as he was my instructor for the NSCAA advanced national course. I learned so much from you in that short week. I was grateful for the opportunity to learn from one of the best, and I am just as grateful for your support of my work.

Because I have gathered so much material over the years from coaches, watching other goalkeepers, and from secondhand information, I would like to extend a sincere apology to any coach or player whose name does not appear with his or her work in reference to the goalkeeping exercises. Last but not least, I am of course grateful to Dr. James A. Peterson and Coaches Choice for publishing my work.

Foreword

Tamara Browder Hageage has written one of the most useful tools for teaching goalkeepers that I have ever come across. A well-respected goalkeeper in her own right, Hageage has produced a manual that is beneficial for all coaches and players who are searching for quality goalkeeper training sessions. The sessions are clear, concise, and well-organized so that anyone with the desire to learn more about the position can grasp the concepts and techniques. Even the most-experienced goalkeepers and goalkeeper coaches will use this book regularly as a reference for new ideas or different ways to coach familiar topics. As a player and coach of the position for 25 years, I've come to realize everyone can spot bad goalkeepers, but not many know how to develop better ones. This book is a must-have for the coaches and players seriously wanting to improve their expertise in goalkeeping.

– Amy (Allmann) Griffin
1991 World Cup champion
U.S. National Team goalkeeping staff coach
University of Washington goalkeeper coach

Contents

Introduction

"There is no substitution for hard work and it is only with persistent, self-disciplined practice that you will improve and achieve consistent performance."

—Peter Shilton, former goalkeeper of England

The two most common complaints I hear from coaches on why they do not take special time to train their goalkeeper are lack of time and/or lack of ideas about what to do. Before every goalkeeping session, I make a coaching outline, just like I would for a team training session. I organize a logical warm-up, decide on my objective, and maintain that focus for the entire session. I understand that this approach can get time-consuming and at times just plain difficult. In this book, I hope to provide coaches and goalkeepers with complete goalkeeper training sessions from warm-up to cooldown. The only choices that will need to be made are what the focus of your training session will be (i.e., catching, low-diving, crosses etc.), and the level of intensity.

If you are a goalkeeper looking for ways to train yourself, fantastic. As a young girl growing up in Toledo, Ohio, finding people who wanted to even kick around for fun was difficult. I trained mostly by myself. I would go behind a local junior high school to my favorite patch of grass and train myself by kicking or throwing a ball against a brick wall. Thus, if you feel your coach is not giving you enough training at practice, then you must take the initiative. Self-motivation is one of a goalkeeper's greatest assets. The position you play on the field is as unique as it is important. Grab a teammate after practice or meet up with a girlfriend or boyfriend. Your mom, dad, sister, or brother could turn out to be a wonderful trainer. My father would sometimes help me train or even warm me up before a game. Although he never played the game himself, he did have the fiercest left-footed toe punch. Those times with him are some of the most treasured moments of my playing career. The bottom line is that the person with you does not need to be a great player, just able to throw and/or kick a ball.

Each session begins with an appropriate warm-up of footwork and ball gymnastics followed by two technical exercises. Each session ends with fitness and strength training. In my opinion, a goalkeeper's ability to communicate is the most important characteristic of the position; however, footwork is a close second. No matter how great the goalkeeper is with her hands, she will not be in the position to use them without solid footwork. Ball gymnastics are wonderful for improving and maintaining flexibility, orientation, and balance. Obviously, the fitter and stronger a goalkeeper, the better equipped she is to use her talents, not to mention reduce her risk of injury. Although not noted after each session, stretching well after any workout is a must. Flexibility can be most improved after a workout because the muscles are warm. Angie Taylor, a certified athletic trainer, has written a wonderful five-minute stretching routine (Appendix A), and Coach Darin Lovat, a professional strength coach, has written a useful piece on the benefits of strength training (Appendix B). Both will be a great aid in helping goalkeepers reduce the risk of injury and be the best they can be.

The following training sessions will be grouped by technical focus. Each session is designed to last approximately 30 to 50 minutes, assuming you are training with two goalkeepers and a coach or trainer. Nearly all of the exercises in this book can be executed with one server (a coach or trainer) and two goalkeepers. When two servers are needed, the non-working goalkeeper is used as the other server.

Although the key coaching points for the technique being trained are noted with each exercise, the focus of this book is not to teach technique. That said, even the most experienced goalkeepers, trainers, or coaches can benefit from review. After all, the basic technical points of goalkeeping are our foundation to greatness. Always remember: practice makes permanent. The primary focus of this book goes hand in hand with the purpose, namely to equip the goalkeeper, coach, or trainer with complete training sessions.

It is important to choose your session based on your level (if you are training yourself), or the level of the goalkeeper with whom you are working. The goalkeeping techniques chart that follows illustrates the basic qualities you should stress in your training sessions for each level (beginning, intermediate, or advanced). Once you or your goalkeeper can perform all of the basic techniques in the appropriate column, you can focus on the next level. In addition to choosing the appropriate level, you will also need to tailor your session to accommodate your goalkeeper's age and fitness level by adjusting the number of repetitions or time duration and the amount of rest between sets. For consistency purposes, all sessions in this book were designed for a fit intermediate goalkeeper age 16, in respect to number of sets, repetitions, and time intervals.

One final note on training: always train the position and not the drill. Inevitably a bad serve will occur. The goalkeeper should always make the technically correct save. For example, you are working on dealing with shots below the waist and the ball is served above the waist. As a rule of thumb, the goalkeeper should use her hands when the ball is above the waist and the scoop or the tuck technique if the ball is below the waist. Training time is precious and should be used wisely

Having goalkeeping training sessions already prepared should take some of the work out of training and leave more time for development and fun. Good luck with your goalkeeping training.

Goalkeepers Techniques Chart

Beginner	Intermediate	Advanced
Fitness	*Fitness*	*Fitness*
• Flexibility • Upper- and lower-body strength • Mid-section strength • Coordination training (balance orientation, reactions, rhythm, footwork)	• Skills listed in the beginner column • Jumping power and speed • Aerobic endurance	• Skills listed in the beginner and intermediate columns • Maximum aerobic fitness
Technique	*Technique*	*Technique*
• Competent field skills training • Catching/receiving balls high and low • Basic positioning and angle play • Diving for low balls • Distribution-punting, throwing, and bowling • Safely dealing with a 1v1	• Skills listed in the beginner column • Tipping over the crossbar • Boxing and catching crosses • Distribution: goal kick and drop kick • Dealing with the back pass • Power-diving and diving forward	• Skills listed in the beginner and intermediate columns • Make practice as realistic as possible to continue perfecting all techniques.
Tactics	*Tactics*	*Tactics*
• Build confidence through safe technique. • Only correct major mistakes. • Do not dwell on details. • Train basic communication such as "keeper," "away," and "man on." • Build confidence and love for the position.	• Skills listed in the beginner column • Teach communication for leadership and better understanding of the defensive shape. • Train on becoming the first line of attack by making better distribution decisions. • Prepare her to maintain mental focus for entire 90 minutes. • Encourage her to accept the responsibility of the position.	• Stress importance of details. • Train technical and tactical situations together. • Improve skills listed in the beginner and intermediate columns at a more intense level (when age is appropriate).

Figure Key

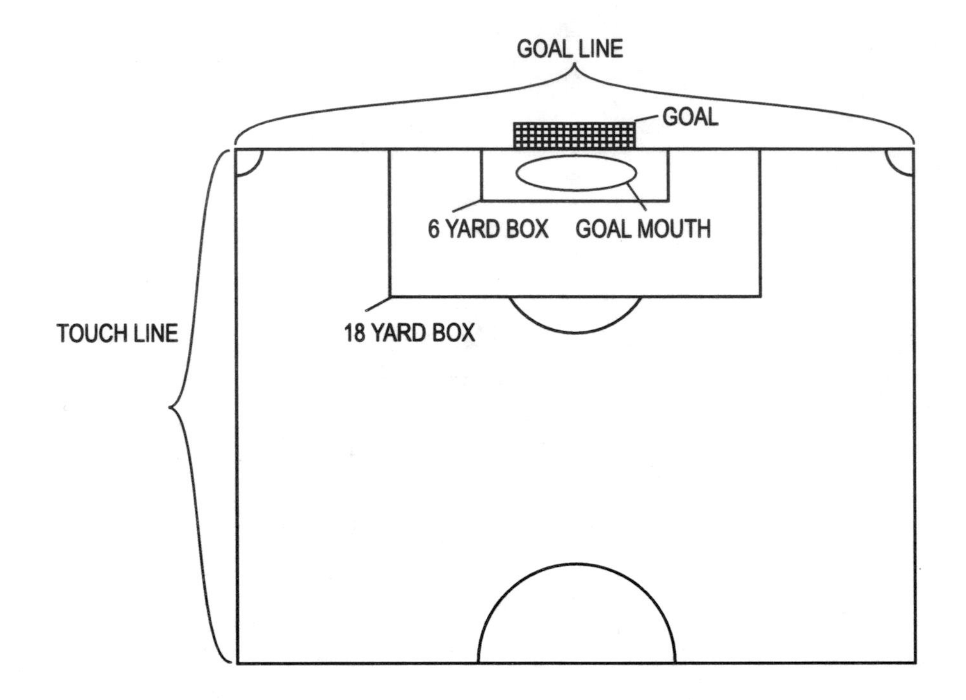

○ = CONE

● = BALL

- - - → = BALL MOVEMENT

——→ = GOALKEEPER/PLAYER MOVEMENT

GK = GOALKEEPER

NWGK = NONWORKING GOALKEEPER

S = SERVER

X = DEFENDING FIELD PLAYER

O = OFFENSIVE FIELD PLAYER

Catching/Hands

CHEST HEIGHT

Equipment Needed: Three cones, 12 balls

Key Coaching Points: For chest-height shots, watch for hand placement behind the ball, with fingers spread. Make sure the goalkeeper catches the ball away from her body, with a slight bend in her elbows to help cushion the ball.

Warm-Up Activities

□ Footwork

Place three cones in a row with eight yards between each cone. Have them perform each of the following exercises three times. Stretch and rest as needed between exercises.

- The goalkeepers start at cone 1 and jog to cone 3, and then back to cone 1.
- The goalkeepers face each other on opposite sides of cone 2. On "go," they shuffle to cone 1, then cone 3, and then back to cone 2 (see Figure 1-1).
- The goalkeepers face each other on opposite sides of cone 2. On "go," they shuffle to cone 1, quick turn to sprint to cone 3, and then shuffle back to cone 2.

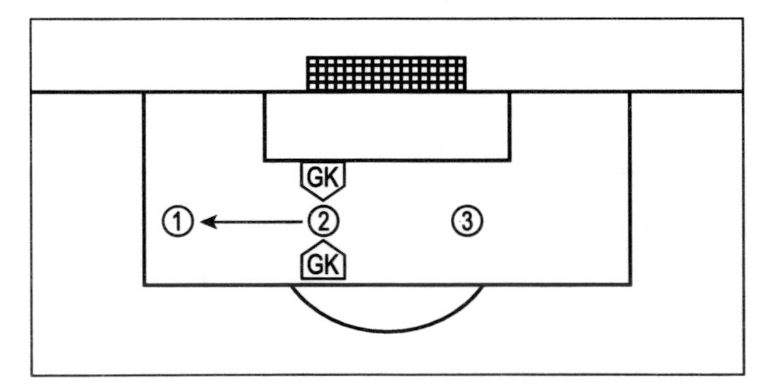

Figure 1-1

- The goalkeepers stand facing cone 3 on opposite sides of cone 2. On "go," they backpedal to cone 1, quick sprint to cone 3, and then backpedal to cone 2.

□ Ball Gymnastics

Have the keeper perform two sets of each exercise at 30-second intervals. Rest and stretch as needed between each exercise.

- Each goalkeeper has a ball. The goalkeeper bounces the ball on the ground with both hands and then catches the ball with both hands. Keeping the feet planted, each player continues to bounce the ball while twisting as far as she can go to one side, and then continues by twisting to the other side.
- Each goalkeeper has a ball. With legs spread slightly more than shoulder-width apart, each player bounces the ball between her legs, and then quickly turns around to catch the ball.

Safe Hands

Have them perform one set of 10 repetitions for each exercise.

- The working goalkeeper stands in the goal, bouncing on the balls of her feet and ready to catch the ball. The non-working goalkeeper stands in front of the goalkeeper, facing her, and is also bouncing on the balls of her feet. The server is approximately 8 to 12 yards away with a supply of balls. On the server's command, the non-working goalkeeper steps out of the way while the server strikes the ball, chest height, at the goalkeeper. If the goalkeeper bobbles the ball and loses possession, the non-working goalkeeper shoots the ball at the goalkeeper again (see Figure 1-2).
- Use the same setup as in the previous exercise, except the goalkeeper begins each rep with her back to the non-working goalkeeper and the server.

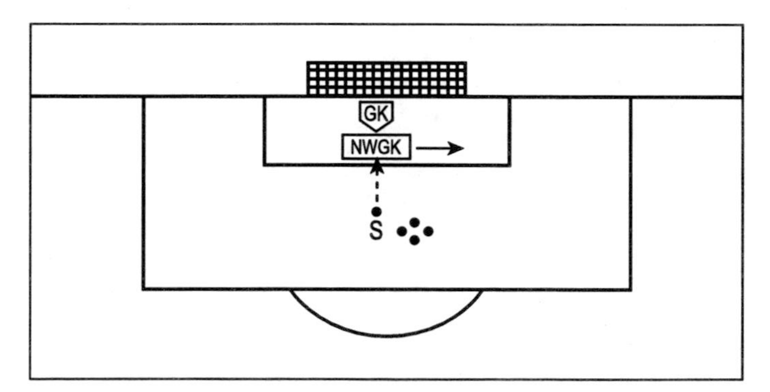

Figure 1-2

- Use the same set up as in the previous exercise, except the goalkeeper starts each rep in a push-up position, with her head on the same side as the non-working goalkeeper and server.
- Use the same set up as in the previous exercise, except the goalkeeper starts each rep on her back, with her feet on the same side as the non-working goalkeeper and server.

Catching with Footwork

Have them perform two sets of 10 repetitions. *Coaching Notes: Make sure the goalkeeper is set solid with equal balance on each leg. Always insist that she hold onto the ball.*

- In the goalmouth, approximately three yards from the goal line, place three cones one yard apart. The server stands around the top right corner of the six-yard box and the non-working goalkeeper stands on the other corner, each with five balls. The goalkeeper starts on the side of the server (see Figure 1-3). The server volleys or throws a hard, chest-height shot at the goalkeeper. The goalkeeper makes the save, tosses the ball back to the server, and then quickly shuffles in and out of the three cones. As soon as the goalkeeper is in a "set" position and ready to receive another shot, the non-working goalkeeper strikes a hard, chest-height shot at the goalkeeper. The exercise continues until the desired number of repetitions is achieved.
- Use the same set up as the previous exercise, except after the goalkeeper tosses the ball back to the server, she laterally jumps with her feet together over each cone.

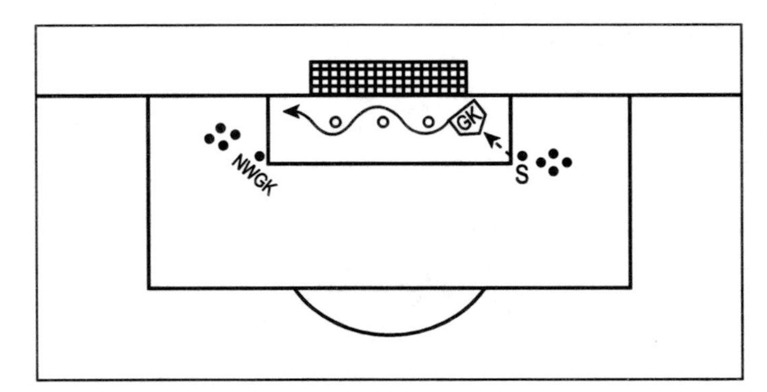

Figure 1-3

Strength/Fitness

Manual Bench Press: The working goalkeeper lays flat on her back with a ball in her hands and her arms up and slightly bent. The other goalkeeper stands over her and puts pressure on the ball. The working goalkeeper resists (see Figure 1-4). Have them perform one set of 10 at an eight-second count.

Leg Scissor: The goalkeeper sits on the ground with a ball. She raises her legs about six inches off the ground and leans backward slightly to find her balance. She then weaves the ball in and out of her legs. She should keep her legs as straight as possible (see Figure 1-5). Have her perform two sets of 25 repetitions.

Figure 1-4

Figure 1-5

TRAINING SOFT HANDS

Equipment Needed: Six balls

Key Coaching Points: As with all catching exercises, sound is the best indicator of proper technique. If there is a loud sound when she receives a ball, her hands are too rigid. Softly meeting, receiving, and cushioning the ball will produce less sound and increase the keeper's success in holding on to the ball.

Warm-Up Activities

□ Footwork

For the following exercises, each goalkeeper has a ball. Have them perform each exercise once for one minute. Stretch and rest as needed between exercises.

- Using the width of the field, the goalkeepers slowly jog while bouncing a ball on the ground and catching it with both hands.
- Same idea as the previous exercise, except this time they shuffle and bounce the ball, again catching the ball with two hands.
- Using the width of the field, the goalkeepers slowly jog while passing the ball from one hand to the other. On command they toss the ball between their legs, and then quickly turn and retrieve the ball.

□ Ball Gymnastics

Under and Over: The two goalkeepers stand back to back, about two feet away from each other, with their legs shoulder-width apart. One goalkeeper starts out with a ball. They both bend over and the one without the ball takes the ball through her legs from the other goalkeeper's hands. They then arch their backs and the goalkeeper without the ball takes the ball over her head from the other's hands. Have them perform two sets of 10. *Coaching Notes: Make sure the players keep their eyes on the ball, always use two hands, and take the ball from each other. On the second set, have them switch roles so the one who gave the ball bending over now gives the ball arching back.*

The Twist: The goalkeepers stand back to back with their legs shoulder-width apart. One has a ball in her hands. Keeping their feet planted, they turn to the same side and pass off the ball, and then quickly turn to the other side, continuing to pass the ball off using two hands. Have them perform two sets of 10.

Soft Hands

Standing: The goalkeeper starts on the goal line in a ready position. The server stands in front of the goalkeeper. Using two balls is most effective, but if the server cannot perform the exercise with two balls, just use one ball. The server tosses a ball right below the goalkeeper's knee. The goalkeeper, using only the hand nearest to the ball, brings her hand out to meet the ball, cushions the ball for control, and then tosses it back to the server (see Figure 2-1). The server should alternate sides. Have them perform two sets of 20.

Moving: The goalkeeper again starts on the goal line in a ready position with the server facing her. Using two balls, the server backs away from the goalkeeper. The goalkeeper must perform the same task described for the standing exercise, this time while moving forward (see Figure 2-2). The server should go as fast as the goalkeeper can go. Once the goalkeeper reaches the top of the 18-yard box, she should then move backward. Have them perform two sets to the top of the 18-yard box and back. *Coaching Notes: Make sure the goalkeeper aggressively steps toward the ball. When she's moving backward, be sure that the goalkeeper stays balanced on the balls of her feet.*

Figure 2-1

Figure 2-2

Shoulder Tap: The server stands at the side of the goalkeeper, holding a ball. The goalkeeper does not look at the server or the ball. The server gently tosses the ball so that it hits the goalkeeper's shoulder. As soon as the goalkeeper feels the ball touch her shoulder, she quickly turns and tries to catch the ball with the furthest hand from the ball (see Figures 2-3 and 2-4). Have her perform one set of 12 on each side. *Coaching Notes: The goalkeeper should turn at the waist and catch the ball from underneath. Challenge her to catch the ball as low to the ground as possible.*

Figure 2-3

Figure 2-4

Across the Body: The server stands at the side of the goalkeeper, holding the ball. The goalkeeper does not look at the server or the ball. The server tosses the ball across the goalkeeper's body just above her waist. The goalkeeper uses the hand furthest away from the server to receive the ball (see Figure 2-5). Have them perform one set of 12 on each side.

Keeper in the Middle

The goalkeeper stands in a ready position between the two servers. Each server should be about three yards away from the goalkeeper and have two balls. Using a drop kick, or striking the ball from the ground, the servers should alternate above-the-waist serves to the goalkeeper. After the goalkeeper saves a shot, she tosses the ball back to the server, and then quickly turns to the other server for the next ball. Have her perform three sets of 10. Coaching Notes: Make sure the keeper meets the ball with her hands behind the ball, and that she cushions and tucks the ball in her arms after every save.

Fitness/Strength

Roll-Out Push-Ups: The goalkeeper starts out with her legs shoulder-width apart, her upper body bent down, and her hands on a ball midway between her feet. She rolls forward on the ball until her body is in a push-up position. She performs a push-up and then, without taking her hands off the ball or going down on her knees, she rolls back into the starting position (see Figure 2-6). Have her perform one set of 10.

Figure 2-5

Figure 2-6

Hungarian Sit-Ups: The goalkeepers sit close on the ground facing opposite directions and so that their hips are in line. Interlocking hands, and keeping their legs straight and off the ground, they bring their legs up and around to the other side (see Figure 2-7). Have them perform two sets of 25.

Figure 2-7

TRAINING STRONG HANDS

Equipment Needed: Six balls

Key Coaching Points: Very little sound is the best indication of good catching technique. Hands should be behind the ball with fingers spread. Make sure she is receiving the ball away from her body, with a slight bend in her elbows, in order to give room to cushion the ball.

Warm-Up Activities

□ Fast Footwork

Have the keepers perform one set of each exercise at 30-second intervals. Stretch and rest as needed between each exercise.

- The goalkeeper stands with her feet shoulder-width apart on points 1 and 2, jumps forward and brings her legs together at point 3, then jumps forward again and lands with feet shoulder-width apart on points 4 and 5. She then jumps backward and brings feet together on point 3, jumps backward again and lands with feet shoulder-width apart on points 1 and 2 (see Figure 3-1).

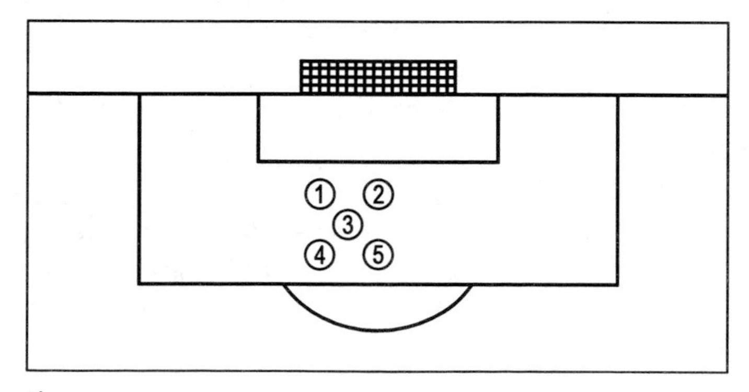

Figure 3-1

- Use the same idea as in the previous exercise, except when jumping forward or backward to point 3, only the right foot touches.
- Use the same idea as in the previous exercise, except when jumping forward or backward to point 3, only the left foot touches.
- Use the same idea as in the first exercise, except once on points 4 and 5 the goalkeeper does a half turn landing on points 4 and 5 again before continuing. Once back to points 1 and 2, again a quick half turn before continuing to point 3.

□ Ball Gymnastics

Stretch and rest as needed after the following exercises.

- The goalkeeper stands with feet more than shoulder-width apart and weaves a ball on the ground in and out of her legs in a figure-eight pattern. Have her perform one set at 20 seconds in each direction.
- The goalkeeper stands with feet shoulder-width apart. Bent over with both hands on the ball, she tosses the ball between her legs, and then quickly moves her arms to the back of her legs to catch the ball before it hits the ground. Have her perform two sets of 12 repetitions.

Catching Circuit

Have the keeper perform two sets of 12 repetitions for each exercise. *Coaching Notes: Make sure when she receives the ball that she is set firmly with equal weight on each leg. When catching above the head, make sure that she catches the ball at the highest point and that it is far enough in front of her that she can always see it. Her wrists should be slightly bent so if she cannot hold on to the ball, the ball will fall in front of her and ideally give her a second chance to gain possession.*

- The goalkeeper is sitting on the ground with her legs straight and spread wide, and her hands resting on her thighs. The server, who is standing a yard away, firmly tosses the ball so it hits the ground between the goalkeeper's legs, level with her knees. As soon as the ball hits the ground, the goalkeeper reacts and catches the ball (see Figure 3-2). *Coaching Note: This exercise is a great technical warm-up for the hands.*
- The goalkeeper kneels on the ground and the server, who is standing five to six yards away, strikes a ball at face or chest level. Serves should steadily increase in velocity. (see Figure 3-3). *Coaching Note: The kneeling position forces the goalkeeper to use her hands and arms, instead of relying on the balance and strength of her legs.*
- The goalkeeper is standing bouncing on the balls of her feet with her hands at her side. The server, who is standing four to six yards away, firmly strikes a ball at face or chest level.

- The goalkeeper is standing bouncing on the balls of her feet with her hands at her side. The server, who is standing four to six yards away, firmly strikes a ball right above her head, high enough so that the goalkeeper's arms must completely extend, but she does not need to jump.

Figure 3-2

Figure 3-3

Hot Pepper

The goalkeepers stand eight yards apart, facing each other. They take turns drop-kicking or volleying a ball to each other. Play three games. The first goalkeeper with three points wins. The loser does 25 push-ups. *Coaching Notes: If your goalkeepers have not yet mastered the drop kick or volley, have them throw the ball at each other. Since the focus of the session is strong hands, all serves should be waist height or above.*

Rules:

- The goalkeeper cannot move out of the way of the kick.
- If the ball touches the goalkeeper and she fails to catch the ball, the other goalkeeper gets a point.

Strength/Fitness

Hand Slaps: The goalkeepers, with gloves off, face each other in a push-up position. On "Go," they each try to slap the other's hand. Their backs should stay straight and they should not go down on their knees (see Figure 3-4). Perform two sets at 30-second intervals. Give them at least 30 seconds rest between each set.

Goalkeeper Sit-Ups: The goalkeepers lay on their backs with feet touching. Using one ball, they take turns throwing the ball back and forth, doing a sit-up every time they catch the ball (see Figure 3-5). Have them perform two sets of 25.

Figure 3-4

Figure 3-5

DEALING WITH BALLS AT WAIST HEIGHT

Equipment Needed: Two cones and six balls

Key Coaching Points: The tuck technique is normally used when dealing with balls at waist height. Make sure she keeps her legs apart for balance. She should receive the ball with outstretched arms and cushion it by bending over. Her head should be over the ball, and her elbows as close together as possible.

Warm-Up Activities

□ Rhythm Exercises

Place two cones or two balls two to three feet apart. Have the keeper perform two sets at 30-second intervals for each exercise. Stretch and rest as needed between each exercise. *Coaching Notes: Rhythm exercises will help improve your goalkeepers' timing and coordination.*

- The goalkeeper goes over cone 1 with the leg nearest to the cone, knees coming up high, and then over cone 2. She then goes back over cone 2, then over cone 2 again, back over cone 2, then back over cone 1, and so on. The rhythm pattern is 1, 2, 2, 2, 2, 1, 1, 1, 1, 2, 2, 2 and so on (see Figure 4-1).
- Same pattern as the previous exercise, except this time the goalkeeper performs the exercise with legs together and laterally jumps.

□ Ball Gymnastics

Have the keepers perform two sets of 12 of each exercise. Stretch and rest between sets as needed.

- Each goalkeeper has a ball. They toss the ball straight up above their head and then catch the ball behind their backs. *Coaching Notes: Challenge them to throw the ball higher and higher. The trick to catching the ball behind your back is not to bend over.*

Figure 4-1

- Each goalkeeper has a ball. They hold the ball above and behind their head arching their back slightly. They drop the ball then quickly bend down to catch the ball by reaching between their legs.

The Tuck

The working goalkeeper stands in front of a three-yard goal. The server and the non-working goalkeeper stand three yards from the goalkeeper to form a triangle. The goalkeeper quickly alternates from server to server, receiving waist-height serves (see Figures 4-2 through 4-4). Have them perform two sets of 12 repetitions for each exercise.

- The servers give a firm underhand serve at the goalkeeper's knees.
- The servers bounce the ball hard a foot from the goalkeeper.
- The servers volley the ball.

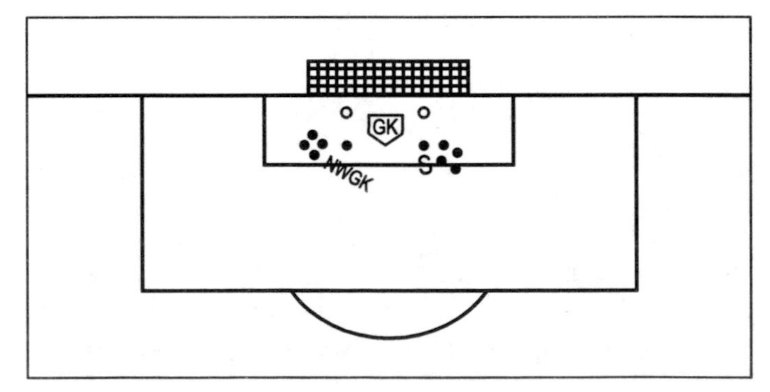

Figure 4-2

Figure 4-3

Figure 4-4

Give and Go

Have the keepers perform two sets of 10 for each exercise.

- The working goalkeeper begins the exercise standing on the outside of the three-yard goal. The server and the non-working goalkeeper stand facing each other and are positioned in the center of the goal three yards from the goal line. The goalkeeper comes forward in ready position, shuffles to the center of the goal, quickly sets to receive a waist-high shot from the server, returns the ball to the server, and quickly turns to go through the cones and set for the second server. After the second save, the goalkeeper returns the ball and shuffles to the other side of the goal, quickly turns, and begins the sequence again (see Figure 4-5).
- Use the same setup as in the previous exercise, except this time the goalkeeper carries a ball in her hands. Once she is set for a shot, she tosses the server a ball in the air right as the server strikes a waist-high shot.

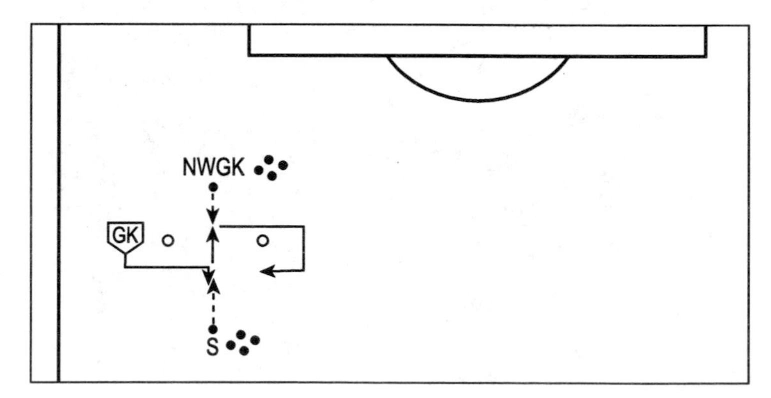

Figure 4-5

Fitness/Strength

Goalkeeper Biceps: The working goalkeeper is on her knees with a ball in her hands, and her elbows pointing down and bent. The non-working goalkeeper tries to push the ball down while the goalkeeper tries to resist (see Figure 4-6). Have them perform one set of eight at an eight-second count.

J-Hawk Abs: Each goalkeeper has a medicine ball (or a soccer ball if you do not have a medicine ball). The goalkeepers begin on their backs with outstretched arms holding the ball in the air. On command, they come up to a 45-degree angle and hold that position until told to go back down (see Figure 4-7). Have them perform two sets of 15 repetitions.

Figure 4-6

Figure 4-7

DEALING WITH SHOTS BELOW THE WAIST

Equipment Needed: Eight cones and eight balls

Key Coaching Points: The goalkeeper should come from behind the ball. If it is an easy ball to handle, she can bend at the waist (see Figure 5-1). Her legs only need to be close enough together so that the ball cannot fit through. If it is a difficult ball or weather conditions are poor, she should kneel flat so that the knee of the leg furthest from the ball almost touches the heel of the foot closest to the ball (see Figure 5-2). In both techniques, she should always step through, come forward, and safely tuck the ball away in her arms.

Warm-Up Activities

- Footwork

Place eight balls or cones in a row, two to three feet apart. Have the keeper perform each exercise three times up and back. Stretch and rest as needed between each exercise.

Figure 5-1

Figure 5-2

High Knees: The starting position is facing the cones. At speed, the goalkeeper goes over each cone, bringing her knees up high and taking one quick step between each cone. Once at the end, she should backpedal to the starting point.

In and Out: The starting position is to the side of the cones. With a slight bend to the knees, while balancing on the balls of her feet, the goalkeeper should weave in and out of the cones, keeping her hips square, head up, eyes forward, and hands ready (see Figure 5-3).

Figure 5-3

Up and Over: The starting position is to the side of the cones. The leg nearest to the cone goes over first and then the second leg follows. With her knees coming up high, the goalkeeper should go up and over each cone, keeping her hips square, head up, eyes forward, and hands ready. Her feet should not touch or cross each other (see Figure 5-4).

□ Ball Gymnastics

- The goalkeeper stands with her legs more than shoulder-width apart and a ball in her hands. In a figure-eight pattern she weaves the ball at knee height between her legs. Perform two sets at 20-second intervals and rest for 20 to 40 seconds between sets.
- The goalkeeper stands with a ball in her hands and her legs shoulder-width apart. The goalkeeper bounces the ball between her legs, and then quickly moves her hands to catch the ball behind her. Perform two sets of 10.

Figure 5-4

Scoop

Make a small goal with cones three yards wide. The goalkeeper stands in the middle of the small goal just behind the cones. The server is about five yards away. Have them perform two sets of 10 for each exercise.

- The server sends a firm pass to the inside of either cone. The goalkeeper must quickly collect the ball in front of the cone. After a save is made, the keeper should quickly shuffle back to the starting position. As soon as she reaches the middle again, the server can serve the next ball (see Figure 5-5).
- Same situation as in the previous exercise, except the goalkeeper quickly shuffles from behind the cone and then around to meet the shot (see Figure 5-6).

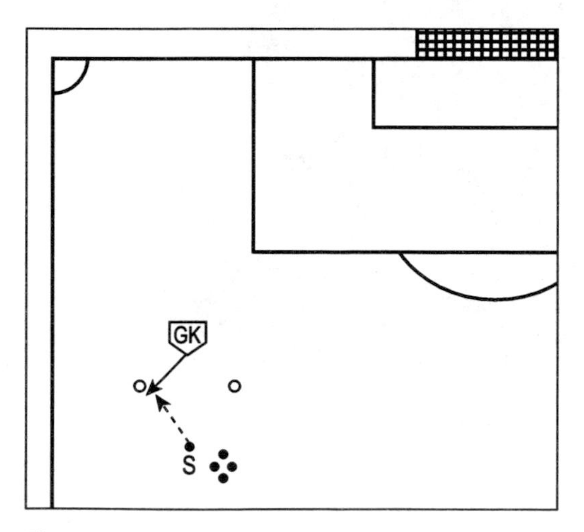

Figure 5-5

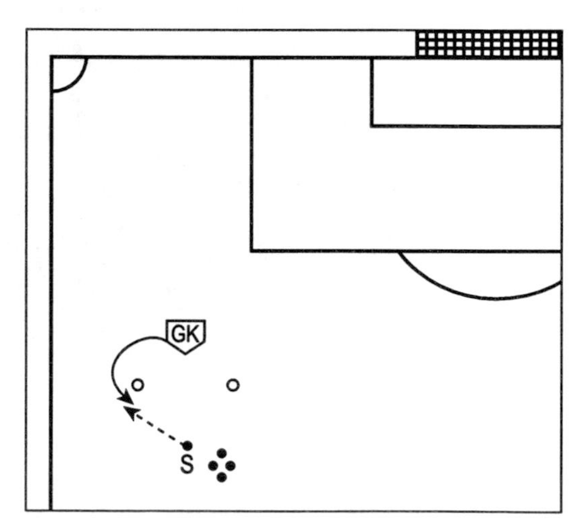

Figure 5-6

Cutthroat

Two one-yard goals are set up eight yards apart. Each goalkeeper is in a goal, and one of them has a ball in her hands. They take turns striking the ball at each other from their goal. A keeper receives a point if the ball hits the front of the other goalkeeper's legs below the knees. The first goalkeeper to three points wins. The loser does 25 push-ups. Play two games.

Fitness/Strength

Goalkeeper Triceps Press: The goalkeepers sit on the ground with their legs extended and feet touching. Using two balls, the first goalkeeper raises herself off the ground by pushing up on the two balls, then lowers her body until she is almost touching the ground, and then repeats this action. Once she has done one set of 10, she rolls the balls to the other goalkeeper and she does a set of 10 (see Figure 5-7). Have her perform two sets of 10.

Four Square Race: Each goalkeeper has an eight-by-eight-yard box marked off with cones. By the first cone place two balls. Taking one ball at a time, the goalkeeper scoops up a ball and sprints to the second cone then sprints back to the first cone to get the second ball. Once she places the second ball next to the first ball, she quickly scoops up the first ball and sprints to the third cone. She continues this process until she is back to the starting position with both balls. Both goalkeepers should go at the same time. The loser does 20 sit-ups. Have them perform this race twice.

Figure 5-7

RECEIVING BALLS AT ALL LEVELS

Equipment Needed: Four cones and eight balls

Key Coaching Points: Refer to key coaching points in Sessions #1 through #5.

Warm-Up Activities

□ Plyometric Circuit

Perform two sets at 20-second intervals for each exercise. Rest and stretch as needed between each exercise. *Coaching Notes: The goalkeepers should stay balanced by having a slight bend at the knees and their weight on the balls of their feet.*

- Each goalkeeper stands behind a ball. On "Go," they quickly tap the top of the ball with their right foot, knee coming up high, followed by their left foot, non-stop. The ball should remain stationary.
- Each goalkeeper stands beside a ball. On "Go," they quickly jump laterally with legs together over the ball and back, non-stop.
- Each goalkeeper stands behind a ball. On "Go," they quickly jump with legs together forward and back over the ball, non-stop.

□ Ball Gymnastics

Stretch and rest as needed between each exercise.

- The goalkeeper stands with legs together and holds the ball in both hands behind her knees. She then tosses the ball up, quickly claps her hands in front of her legs, and then quickly reaches back to catch the ball before it hits the ground. Have her perform two sets of 10.
- The goalkeeper stands with the ball held up by her face. She circles her head with the ball 10 times in one direction, and then 10 times the other way. She then does the same around her waist, and then her closed legs. Have her perform two sets of 10 in both directions.

Square Work

Set up a 10-by-10-yard grid. Have the keepers perform one set of 10 for each exercise. *Coaching Notes: Because of the close proximity of the serves, adjust the weight of the serve so the goalkeeper can consistently perform each exercise with the proper technique. Once she has mastered the technique, increase the weight of the serve. Always train technique before power.*

- Goalkeepers move in all directions, jogging, skipping, shuffling, backpedaling, and so on. The server who stands in the middle of the grid with a ball calls out a name. The goalkeeper who has been called receives a firm shot on the ground right at her feet. After scooping the ball, she gives the ball back to the server and continues moving around in the grid (see Figure 6-1).
- Use the same idea as in the previous exercise, except when the keeper is called she quickly sprints to the nearest cone, touches the cone, and then turns and sets for a waist-high shot.
- Use the same idea as in the previous exercise, except when the keeper is called she quickly performs a low dive to the nearest cone, and then springs up to receive a chest-height or above-the-head shot.

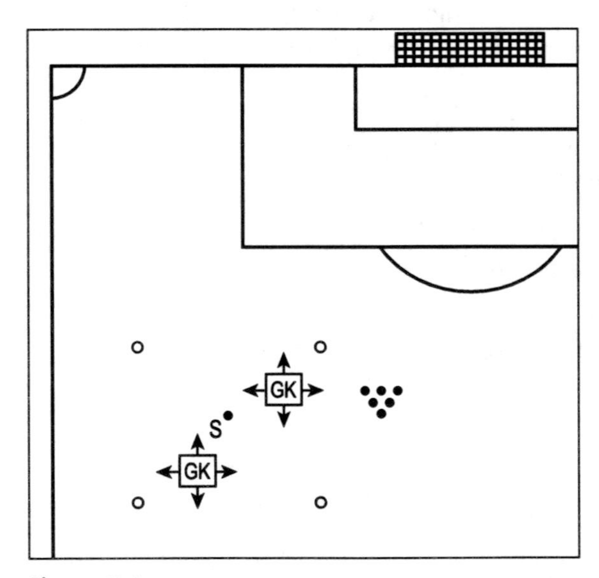

Figure 6-1

Super Eight

The goalkeeper stands with her shoulder on the goalpost facing the sideline. On the server's command, she quickly moves off the post and sets for a shot. The server is around 10 yards away with eight balls lined up. The server should vary the serves to cover ground, waist high, chest height, and right above the head (see Figure 6-2). Have them perform two sets of eight on each side of the goal.

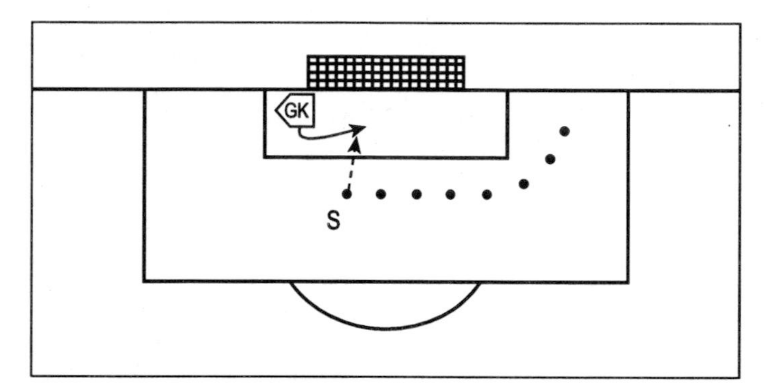

Figure 6-2

Strength/Fitness

Protect Your Baby: One goalkeeper has a ball tucked in her arms. The other goalkeeper may do anything (except spit, punch, tickle, or kick) to get the ball. The keeper holding on to the ball must stand in the same spot. If the non-working goalkeeper gets the ball from the goalkeeper, she gives it right back. The goalkeeper that manages to hold on to her "baby" and loses possession the fewest times wins. Each goalkeeper gets two turns to hold on to the ball for 30 seconds.

Human Hurdles: The goalkeepers lay on their stomachs side by side. Goalkeeper 1 dives over goalkeeper 2, landing on her stomach and using her arms to catch herself. They continue this process until each keeper has gone 10 times. After a one-minute rest, they do a second set back to their original starting position (see Figures 6-3 and 6-4).

Figure 6-3

Figure 6-4

2

Angle Play

CUTTING DOWN THE ATTACKER'S ANGLE

Equipment Needed: Eight cones and eight balls

Key Coaching Points: You can best explain angle play by telling your goalkeeper to visualize a line going from the posts to the ball as shown in Figure 7-1. The closer she gets to the ball, the closer the lines get to her. Thus, a goalkeeper who stands on her goal line for a shot at the top of the 18-yard box has a long way to dive to each post. As she moves closer, the power dive needed at the goal line can be reduced to a reaction save. Your goalkeeper will have to determine how far she is able to come out based on her ability to get back to cover the ground behind her.

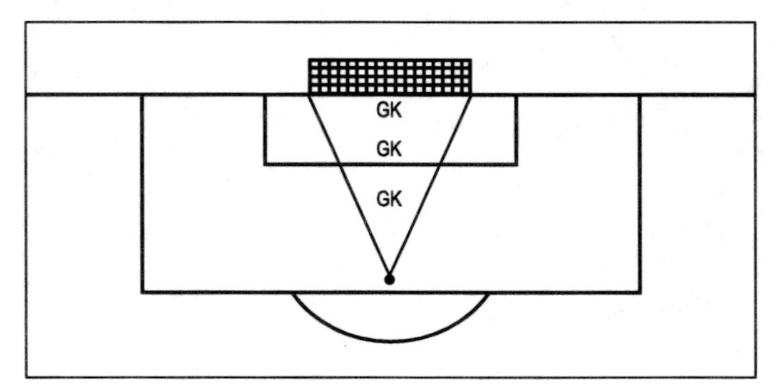

Figure 7-1

Warm-Up Activities

- Footwork

Place eight cones or balls two to three feet apart. For the first three exercises, have the keeper perform three sets of each. Stretch and rest as needed.

In and Out: The starting position is to the side of the cones. With a slight bend in the knees, while balancing on the balls of her feet, the goalkeeper should weave in and out of the cones, keeping her hips square, head up, eyes forward, and hands ready (see Figure 5-1 in Session #5).

Up and Over: The starting position is to the side of the cones. The leg nearest to the cone goes over first and then the second leg follows. With her knees coming up high, the goalkeeper should go up and over each cone keeping her hips square, head up, eyes forward and hands ready. Her feet should not touch or cross (see Figure 5-2 in Session #5).

Extended In and Out: Move every other cone one yard up so the cones make a zigzag pattern. The technique is the same as described in the In and Out exercise, except her first step should be big. The leg closest to the cone should be used to take the first step. Her first step should beat the cone. Be sure the goalkeeper keeps her balance when backpedaling by keeping her weight on the balls of her feet and staying low (see Figure 7-2).

Figure 7-2

□ Goalkeeper Suicides

Place a cone at the six-yard line, the penalty mark, and the top of the 18-yard box. Both goalkeepers begin on the goal line. When ready they sprint to the six-yard line and backpedal to the goal line, then the 12-yard line and backpedal to the goal line, and then the 18-yard line and backpedal to the goal line. Have them perform three sets. Rest and stretch as needed.

□ Ball Gymnastics

Stretch and rest as needed between each exercise.

- The goalkeeper stands with her legs together and the ball in both hands held behind her knees. She then tosses the ball up, quickly claps her hands in front of her legs, and then quickly reaches back to catch the ball. Have her perform two sets of 10.

- The goalkeeper stands with the ball held up by her face. She circles her head with the ball 10 times in one direction and then 10 times the other way. She then does the same around her waist, and then around her closed legs. Have her perform two sets in both directions.

Turn

Randomly place eight balls inside and outside the 18-yard box. The non-working goalkeeper and server stand behind a ball (see Figure 7-3). The goalkeeper begins the exercise on her goal line with her back to the field. When the server says, "Turn," the non-working goalkeeper must take one touch on the ball she is standing behind before she shoots. The goalkeeper quickly approaches the ball after the first touch to cut down the angle of the attacker. After making the save, the goalkeeper returns to her goal line and the non-working goalkeeper says, "Turn" for the server. Have them perform two sets of eight.

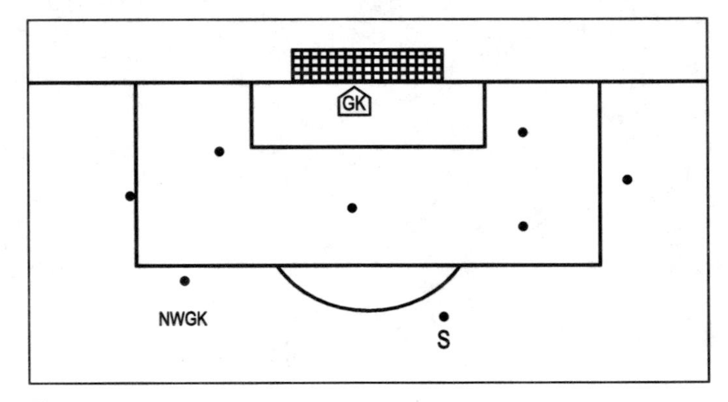

Figure 7-3

50-50

Place eight balls inside and outside the 18-yard box. The non-working goalkeeper and server line up an equal distance from a ball with the goalkeeper (see Figure 7-4). The goalkeeper begins the exercise on her goal line. When the server says, "Go," the goalkeeper, using the time it takes the attacker to get to the ball, approaches the non-working goalkeeper's ball to cut down the angle. The non-working goalkeeper must shoot the ball on her first touch. After making the save, the goalkeeper returns to her goal line and the non-working goalkeeper says "Go" for the server. Have them perform two sets of eight.

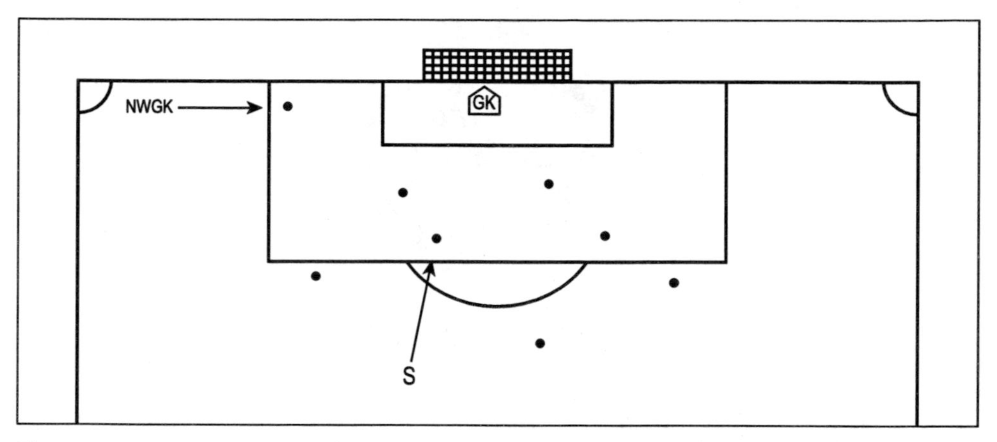

Figure 7-4

Strength/Fitness

Core: The goalkeepers begin the exercise on their hands and knees. Keeping their stomach muscles tight and their backs flat, they slowly raise their right arm and their left leg so that they are parallel with the ground. Hold this position for two seconds and then slowly lower back to the starting position. Have the keepers repeat this movement with the left arm and the right leg. Have them perform one set of 20.

Walking Lunges: The goalkeepers begin this exercise in a standing position with their hands on their hips. They lunge out with their right leg so that the upper part of their right leg is parallel with the ground and their left leg is almost straight. Putting all their weight on their right leg, they push back up into the starting position. Have the keepers repeat this movement with the left leg. Have them perform one set of 12.

RECOVERING

Equipment Needed: Three cones and 12 balls

Key Coaching Points: You can best explain angle play by telling your goalkeeper to visualize a line going from the posts to the ball, as shown in Figure 8-1. The closer she gets to the ball, the closer the lines get to her. Thus, a goalkeeper who stands on her goal line for a shot at the top of the 18-yard box has a long way to dive to each post. As she moves closer, the power dive needed at the goal line can be reduced to a reaction save. Your goalkeeper will have to determine how far she is able to come out based on her ability to get back to cover the ground behind her.

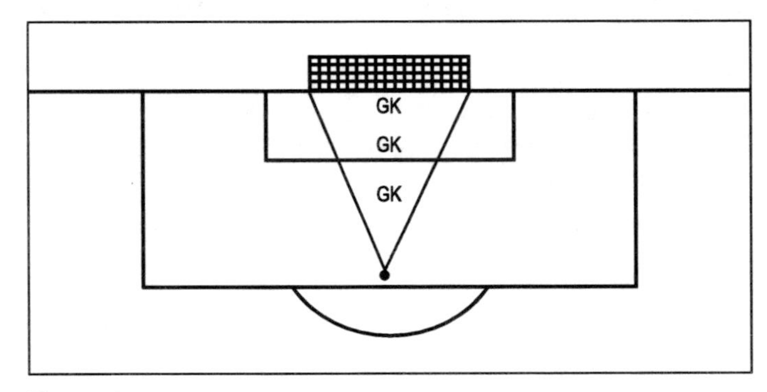

Figure 8-1

Warm-Up Activities

□ Footwork

Place three cones in a row with eight yards between each cone. Perform each exercise three times. Stretch and rest as needed between each set (three times equals one set).

- The goalkeepers start at cone 1 and jog to cone 3.
- The goalkeepers face each other on opposite sides of cone 2. On "Go," they shuffle to cone 1, then cone 3, and then back to cone 2 (see Figure 8-2).

- The goalkeepers face each other on opposite sides of cone 2. On "Go," they shuffle to cone 1, make a quick turn to sprint to cone 3, and then shuffle back to cone 2.
- The goalkeepers stand facing cone 3 on opposite sides of cone 2. On "Go," they backpedal to cone 1, make a quick sprint to cone 3, and then backpedal to cone 2.

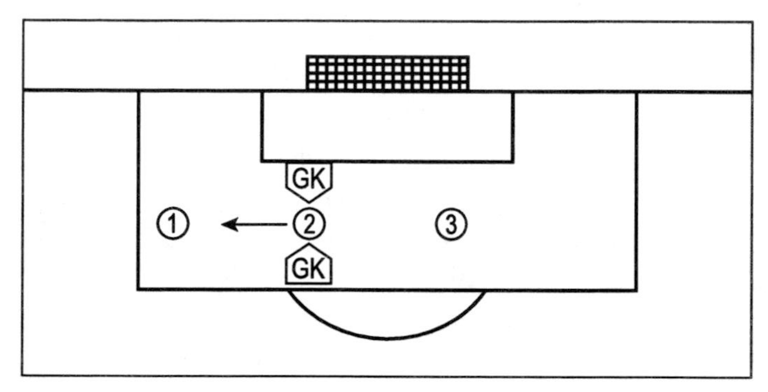

Figure 8-2

□ Ball Gymnastics

Perform one set of six with a one-minute rest period between each set to stretch.

- Each goalkeeper has a ball. They toss the ball up in the air, quickly do a forward roll back to a standing position, and catch the ball before it hits the ground.
- Each goalkeeper has a ball. Sitting on the ground they toss the ball up in the air and quickly stand (without using their hands) to catch the ball before it hits the ground.

Touch and Go

Place a ball seven yards from the goal line. The server and the non-working goalkeeper are at the top of the 18-yard box with a supply of balls. The goalkeeper begins the exercise on her goal line (see Figure 8-3). When ready, she sprints to the ball and

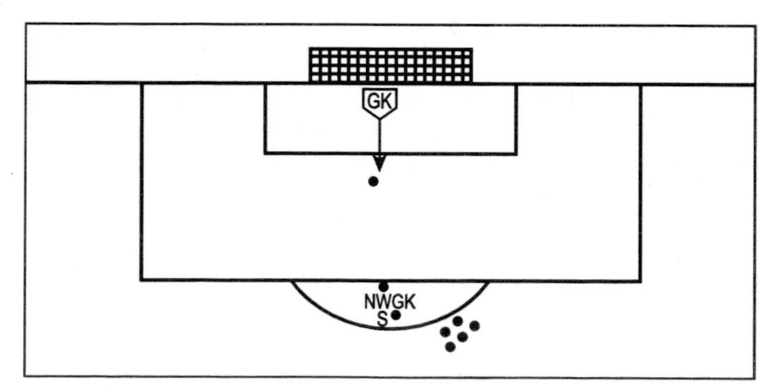

Figure 8-3

touches the ball with a hand. As soon as the ball is touched, the goalkeeper quickly adjusts to the oncoming shot. The attacker must take one heavy touch before the shot. Have them perform three sets of six. Change the location of the stationary ball for each set. *Coaching Notes: For greater challenge, place the stationary ball further away from the goal line.*

Cross and Recover

The non-working goalkeeper is on the left side of the goal with six balls scattered inside and outside of the 18-yard box. The server is outside of the 18-yard box on the right side of the goal with a supply of balls. The goalkeeper begins the exercise at one third to two thirds of the way back in their goal (see Figure 8-4). The server sends a cross either in the air or on the ground. After the goalkeeper saves the cross she quickly recovers to field a shot from the non-working goalkeeper. The non-working goalkeeper must take one heavy touch before the shot. Have them perform two sets of 12. Every cross and shot counts as a repetition.

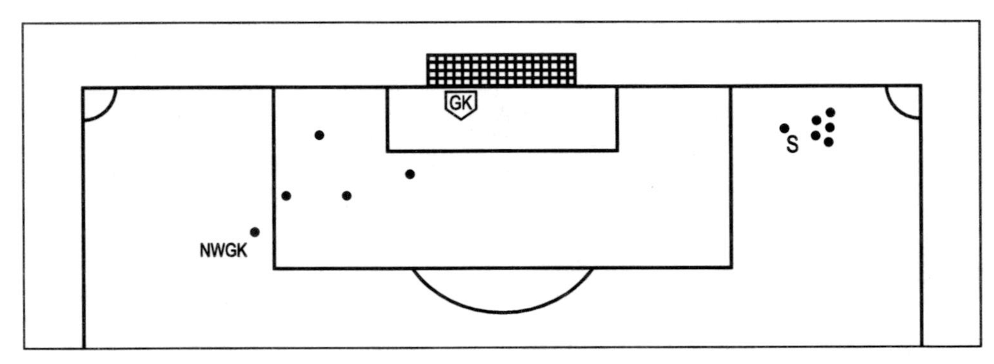

Figure 8-4

Strength/Fitness

Two Ball Balance: With a ball in each hand, the goalkeepers get into a push-up position and balances on the two balls. Have them perform three sets at 30-second intervals.

Goalkeeper Sit-Ups: The goalkeepers lay on their backs with feet touching. Using one ball, they take turns throwing the ball back and forth, doing a sit-up every time they catch the ball (see Figure 3-6 in Session #3). Have them perform two sets of 25 reps.

3

Reactions

ABOVE THE WAIST

Equipment Needed: Two cones and 10 balls

Key Coaching Points: When it comes to a reaction save, good technique is not always possible. The key to quick reactions is to have your goalkeepers keep their weight on the balls of their feet to provide balance and the ability to move in any direction. Stress to the keeper to try to hold on to everything, and if the ball is deflected, to always aggressively chase down all mishandled shots.

Warm-Up Activities

□ Footwork

Using a ball and a cone make an eight-yard goal. The goalkeepers face each other on opposite sides of the goal. Using this setup, the goalkeepers react to the following commands from the server. Have them perform each exercise once at 30-second intervals. Rest and stretch as needed.

- Exercise one: "Right" or "Left"
- Exercise two: if the server says, "Right," the goalkeepers shuffle to their left. It the server says, "Left," the goalkeepers shuffle to their right.
- Exercise three: "Cone" or "Ball"
- Exercise four: if the server says, "Cone," they shuffle to the ball. If the server says, "Ball," they shuffle to the cone.

□ Ball Gymnastics

Stretch and rest as needed between exercises.

Reverse Diving: One goalkeeper is standing with a ball in her hands. The other goalkeeper is lying on the ground on her side. The keeper with the ball tosses the ball up in the air so that the keeper on the ground can quickly get up and catch the ball before it hits the ground. As soon as the keeper with the ball tosses the ball in the air, she quickly dives on the ground, staying on her side as if low-diving on a ball. Make sure they alternate the side on which they dive down. They continue this exercise until each keeper has gone 10 times.

Hike: Each goalkeeper has a ball. Standing with her legs shoulder-width apart, she hikes the ball up between her legs so that the ball comes up and around her back and over her shoulder so she is able to catch the ball. Make sure she alternates the shoulder over which the ball goes. Have her perform one set of 12 repetitions.

Fast Hands

The goalkeeper begins this exercise two yards off her goal line. The server and non-working goalkeeper are at the top of the 18-yard box with a supply of balls. Perform three sets of eight. *Coaching Notes: The attacker must give the command and then take one short touch before she shoots the ball. The shots should be above the waist and right at the goalkeeper.*

- For the first set, the goalkeeper has her back to the field and turns on command from the attacker.
- For the second set, the goalkeeper is in a sitting position facing the field and gets up on command from the attacker.
- For the third set, the goalkeeper is lying flat on her back with her feet pointing toward the attacker and gets up on command from the attacker.

Rapid Fire

Line up 10 balls 12 to 14 yards from the goal line. The goalkeeper begins the exercise in her goalmouth at a comfortable distance from the balls. Without pausing, the server shoots the first five balls, and the non-working goalkeeper finishes the exercise by shooting the next five. The shots should be within one yard of the goalkeeper. Only pause enough between each shot to give the goalkeeper a chance to make the next save. Perform three sets of 10. *Coaching Notes: For added fun, keep score and have the loser do push-ups.*

Strength/Fitness

Manual Bench Press: The working goalkeeper lays flat on her back with a ball in her hands and her arms up and slightly bent. The other goalkeeper stands over her and puts pressure on the ball. The working goalkeeper resists (see Figure 1-4 in Session #1). Have them perform one set of eight at an eight-second count.

30-Yard Sprints: Mark off 30 yards with two cones. Have the keepers perform two sprints in each of the following starting positions:

- Facing the finish line
- Back to the finish line
- Sitting with back to the finish line
- In a push-up position

BELOW THE WAIST

Equipment Needed: Two cones and 10 balls

Key Coaching Points: When it comes to a reaction save, good technique is not always possible. The key to quick reactions is to have your goalkeepers keep their weight on the balls of their feet to provide balance and the ability to move in any direction. Stress to the keeper to try to hold on to everything, and if the ball is deflected to always aggressively chase down all mishandled shots.

Warm-Up Activities

□ Shadow

Make a small six-yard wide goal with two cones. The two goalkeepers stand facing each other on opposite sides of the goal. Pick one goalkeeper to be the leader and the other goalkeeper to be the follower. The leader makes quick movements up, back, side to side, diving to a cone, and jumping. The following goalkeeper shadows the leader's movements. Have the keepers perform four sets at 30-second intervals. Have the goalkeepers change rolls after each set.

□ Pick-Up

The server stands facing the goalkeeper with a ball in each hand. The server randomly drops one ball at a time, giving the goalkeeper just enough time to save the ball and toss it back to the server. The goalkeeper should not let the ball touch the ground. Have her perform two sets of 12.

□ Ball Gymnastics

- The goalkeeper sits on the ground with legs straight and spread wide. She rolls the ball around her feet slowly five times in one direction and then five more times in the opposite direction.

- The goalkeeper sits on the ground with legs straight and spread wide. She twists around and places the ball behind her back, and then twists in the opposite direction to retrieve the ball. Have her do five twists with the ball in both directions.

Forward Roll

The server is 12 yards from the goal line with a supply of balls. The goalkeeper begins the exercise standing on her goal line. When ready, the goalkeeper performs a forward roll and as soon as the server can see the goalkeeper's face she strikes a hard shot right at the goalkeeper. Have her perform two sets of eight.

In Your Face

The goalkeeper begins this exercise a yard off her goal line. The non-working goalkeeper is a yard away from the goalkeeper and is facing her (see Figure 10-1). The two goalkeepers chest pass the ball back and forth as they shuffle from post to post. When the server, who is eight yards away from the goal line, says "Shot," the goalkeeper forgets the ball being passed and reacts to the server's shot. Shots should be within one yard of the goalkeeper. Have them perform two sets of eight.

Strength/Fitness

20-Yard Shuttle Runs: Use two cones to mark of a distance of 20 yards. The goalkeepers start at cone 1, then sprint to cone 2, then back to cone 1, and finish by sprinting back to cone 2 for a total of 60 yards. Have them perform eight shuttle runs where 60 yards equals one set. Use a one-to-three work/rest ratio, or rest as needed.

Leg Lifts with a Ball: Both goalkeepers lay flat on the ground with a ball between their feet and their arms out straight so that the arms are perpendicular to their body. Keeping the ball off the ground and legs straight, they lift the ball with their legs to their hands. They then lower their legs back to the starting position without the ball and then bring their legs back up and put the ball back between their feet. Have them perform two sets of 10.

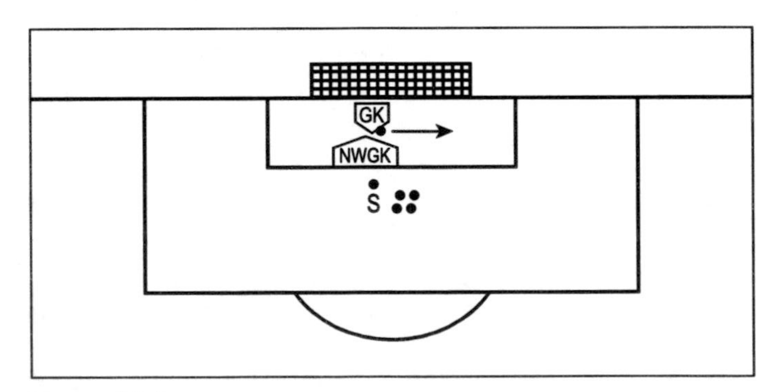

Figure 10-1

MAKING THE SECOND SAVE

Equipment Needed: Eight cones and 10 balls

Key Coaching Points: When it comes to a reaction save, good technique is not always possible. The key to quick reactions is to have your goalkeepers keep their weight on the balls of their feet to provide balance and the ability to move in any direction. Stress to the keeper to try to hold on to everything, and if the ball is deflected to always aggressively chase down all mishandled shots.

Warm-Up Activities

- Star

The goalkeeper begins in the center of the star, which is four yards in each direction from the center spot. She listens for a command from the server to move up, back, right, or left. The goalkeeper always begins and ends in the center of the star. Have the keepers perform each set at 30-second intervals, and stretch and rest as needed between sets (see Figure 11-1).

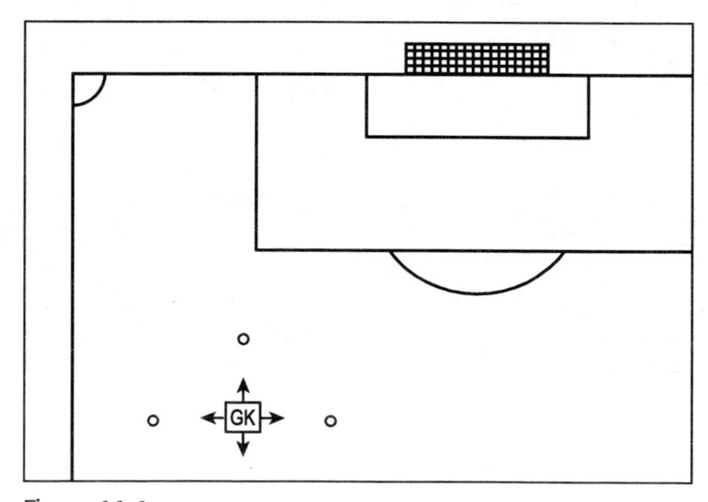

Figure 11-1

- For the first set, the server only gives one command at a time.
- For the second set, the server gives two commands at a time.
- For the third set, the server gives three commands at a time.

□ Keeper in the Middle

The non-working goalkeeper and the server stand six from the goalkeeper so that the goalkeeper is in the middle. The server drives a shot at the goalkeeper's feet. The goalkeeper makes the save and tosses the ball back to the server. She then quickly turns to face another shot from the non-working goalkeeper. Have them perform three sets of 10. For the second set drive the shot at the goalkeeper's knees and for the third set serve the ball at the goalkeeper's chest.

□ Ball Gymnastics

Have the keepers perform one set of 12 repetitions for each exercise and stretch as needed between sets.

- The goalkeeper sits on the ground with her feet up. She rolls the ball down from her feet to her chest and then rocks forward to get the ball back up to her feet. Her feet should never touch the ground and she should not use her hands (see Figure 11-2).
- The goalkeeper sits on the ground with her legs up and a ball in her hands. Keeping her feet up, have her rotate the ball between her legs in a figure-eight pattern (see Figure 11-3).

Figure 11-2

Figure 11-3

Soft Shot, Hard Shot

The non-working goalkeeper stands eight yards off the goal line and off to one side with a supply of balls. The server is 12 yards off the goal line with a supply of balls. The goalkeeper begins in the center of the goalmouth. The first shot comes from the non-working goalkeeper, who serves a ball to the feet of the goalkeeper. As soon as the goalkeeper touches the ball, the server strikes a hard shot within a yard of the goalkeeper's body. Have them perform three sets of 10. Every shot equals one repetition.

Sit and Serve

The non-working goalkeeper is at the right goalpost with a supply of balls. The server is 12 yards off the goal line. Place four balls on the goal line. The goalkeeper begins each repetition by sitting on the goal line and rolling a ball to the server (see Figure 11-4). As soon as the goalkeeper rolls the ball out to the server, she quickly stands up to react to the shot. As soon as the server strikes the first ball, the non-working goalkeeper passes the server a ball for the second shot. Perform three sets of eight. Every shot equals one repetition.

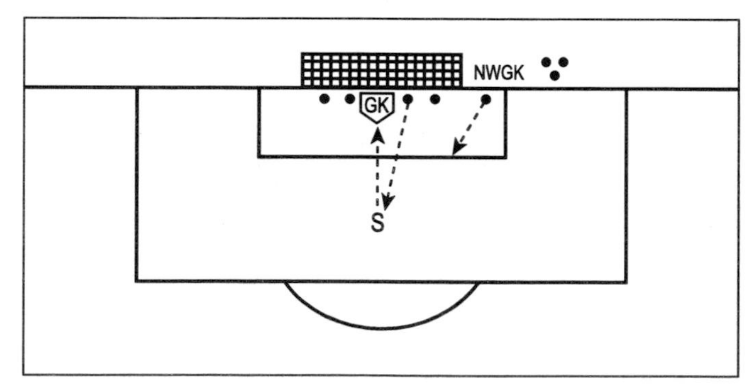

Figure 11-4

Strength/Fitness

Goalkeeper Suicides: Mark off the six-yard line, the 12-yard line, and the 18-yard line with three cones. Both goalkeepers begin on the goal line. They sprint to the six-yard line and backpedal to the goal line, then they sprint to the 12-yard line and backpedal to the goal line, and they finish by sprinting to the 18-yard line and backpedaling to the goal line. Have them perform five sets.

Mountain Climbers: Both goalkeepers begin the exercise in a push-up position. They bring their right knee up toward their chest and leave their left leg straight, then quickly change by bringing their left knee up toward their chest while extending their right leg. Have them perform three intervals of 30 seconds.

CAN I MAKE YOU PUKE?

Equipment Needed: Three cones and 10 balls

Key Coaching Points: When it comes to a reaction save, good technique is not always possible. The key to quick reactions is to have your goalkeepers keep their weight on the balls of their feet to provide balance and the ability to move in any direction. Stress to the keeper to try to hold on to everything, and if the ball is deflected to always aggressively chase down all mishandled shots.

Warm-Up Activities

□ Commando

Both goalkeepers jog in place with a ball in their hands. After each command they quickly return to the jogging in place. They must always perform all commands with the ball in their hands. Have them perform three sets at 30-second intervals. Stretch and rest as needed.

- For the first set, they react to the following commands: shuffle right, shuffle left, or jump.
- For the second set, they react to the following commands: dive right, dive left or push-up (meaning to perform a push-up on the ball).
- For the last set, they react to the following commands: move forward, move backward, or lay flat on your back.

□ Ball Gymnastics

Stretch as needed between each exercise.

Reverse Diving: One goalkeeper is standing with a ball in her hands. The other goalkeeper is lying on the ground on her side. The keeper with the ball tosses the ball up in the air so that the keeper on the ground can quickly get up and catch the ball before it hits the ground. As soon as the keeper with the ball tosses the ball in the air, she quickly dives on the ground, staying on her side as if low-diving to a ball. Make sure they alternate the side on which they dive down. They continue this exercise until each keeper has gone 10 times.

Hike: Each goalkeeper has a ball. Standing with her legs shoulder-width a part, she hikes the ball up between her legs so that the ball comes up and around her back and over her shoulder and she is able to catch the ball. Make sure she alternates the shoulder over which the ball goes. Have her perform one set of 12 repetitions.

1-2-3

Place a ball two yards off the goal line just inside both goal posts (see Figure 12-1). The server is 12 yards out with a supply of balls. The goalkeeper begins the exercise by diving on ball one, then quickly getting up and diving on ball two, then quickly getting up again to react to a shot from the server. The server should drive her shot at or near the goalkeeper. Have them perform two sets of eight.

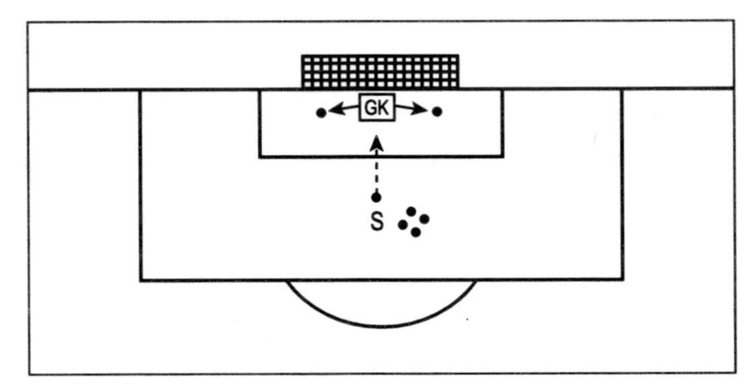

Figure 12-1

Can I Make You Puke?

Make a triangle with three cones placed five yards apart. The goalkeeper begins the exercise in the middle of the triangle, which represents three small goals. The server stands eight yards from one of the small goals with a supply of balls. The non-working goalkeeper stands five yards from a goal with a supply of balls. For the third goal place a ball five yards out (see Figure 12-2). The goalkeeper begins by approaching the stationary ball and smothering it. She then quickly gets up and approaches the non-working goalkeeper who will volley a ball at the goalkeeper just above her head. After the second save, the goalkeeper quickly approaches the server who will shoot a ball either just inside the right or left cone. The goalkeeper then repeats this sequence until the server says, "Stop." Have them perform three sets at 45-second intervals.

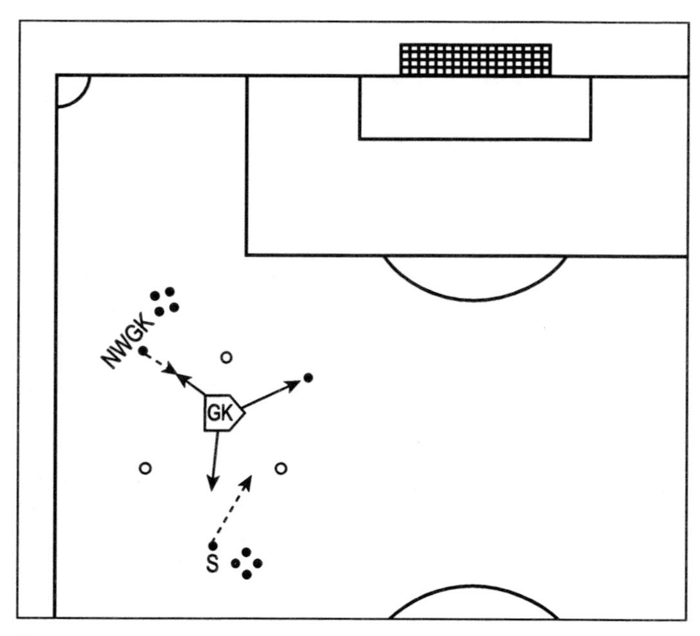

Figure 12-2

Strength/Fitness

Goalkeeper Sit-Ups: The goalkeepers lay on their backs with feet touching. Using one ball, they take turns throwing the ball back and forth, doing a sit-up every time they catch the ball (see Figure 3-5 in Session #3). Have them perform two sets of 25 reps.

Carry Your Partner: One goalkeeper gets on the back of the other goalkeeper who then, moving as quickly as possible, carries her from the goal line to the top of the 18-yard box and back. Have them perform three sets.

4

Low-Diving

NEAR-POST SAVE

Equipment Needed: Two cones and 12 balls

Key Coaching Points: The goalkeeper should land on her side and be sure her top hand is on top of the ball and her bottom hand is behind the ball. Stress the importance of letting the ball hit the ground first to cushion her fall and of using the ground as her third hand. Her bottom arm should come out and away from her body. After the ball, her shoulder—not her elbow—should hit the ground. She should keep her neck steady and straight. She should dive toward the ball at a forward angle and keep her bottom leg slightly bent and on the ground to maintain her balance on her side. When diving low, her bottom hand will have the best reach. She should always use two hands when possible. If she cannot save the shot with two hands, insist that she use a flat palm to redirect the ball out of bounds. The number one rule of diving: only dive when necessary.

Warm-Up Activities

□ Footwork

The goalkeepers perform each exercise in the six-yard box, as shown in Figure 13-1. Have them perform each exercise three times. Rest and stretch as needed between exercises.

- The goalkeeper starts at the right goalpost. On "Go," she quickly shuffles to the left goalpost, then sprints diagonally to cone 1, then shuffles to cone 2, and then backpedals on a diagonal to the right goalpost.
- Use the same progression as in the previous exercise, except have her start at the left goalpost.

□ Ball Gymnastics

Have the keepers perform one set of eight of each exercise. Rest and stretch as needed.

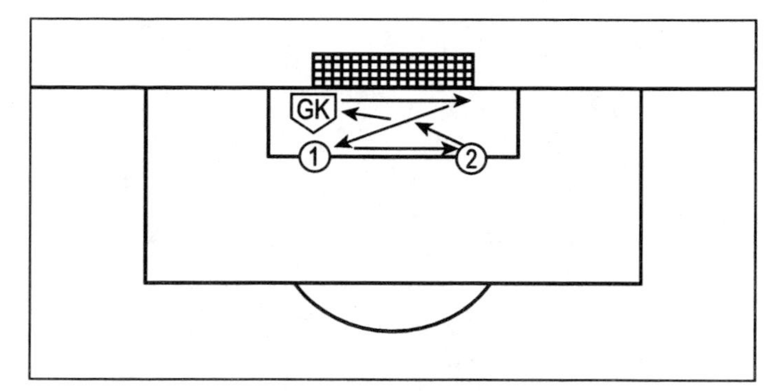

Figure 13-1

- Each goalkeeper has a ball. They toss the ball up in the air, quickly do a forward roll back to a standing position, and catch the ball before it hits the ground.
- Each goalkeeper has a ball. Sitting on the ground they toss the ball up in the air and quickly stand (without using their hands) to catch the ball before it hits the ground.

Low-Diving Circuit

Have the keepers perform one set of 12 for each exercise.

V-Sits: The goalkeeper sits on the ground with her legs out in front of her, as shown in Figures 13-2 and 13-3. The server gives an underhand toss to one side. The goalkeeper dives forward, trying to save the ball up toward her feet, creating a "V" when she saves the ball. *Coaching Notes: V-sits help goalkeepers warm up in two ways. First, they warm up her hands, shoulders, and neck, thus preparing her upper body for the task of diving. Second, they prepare her mentally to always attack the ball and dive toward the ball at a forward angle.*

Figure 13-2

Figure 13-3

Figure 13-4

Kneeling: The goalkeeper kneels on the ground and the server strikes a ball at face or chest level. Serves should steadily increase in velocity (see Figure 13-4). *Coaching Notes: This exercise is great for improving hand and arm strength. The kneeling position forces the keeper to use her hands and arms, instead of relying on the balance and strength of her legs.*

Standing: From a standing position, the goalkeeper performs a low dive using one step (see Figures 13-5, 13-6, and 13-7).

Near Post

The goalkeeper begins in the center of the goal on the goal line. On the servers command, she moves in a controlled manner up and around the cone, which is placed approximately four yards on an angle from the goal line and four yards from the near post. As soon as she is around the cone, she should set to receive a firm shot on the ground right inside the near post. The server should be approximately 10 yards away (see Figure 13-8). Have them perform two sets of eight on each side. *Coaching Notes: Depending on the level and age of your goalkeeper, adjust the distance of the cone away from the goal line (the closer the cone is to the goal and the post, the easier the exercise).*

Figure 13-5

Figure 13-6

Figure 13-7

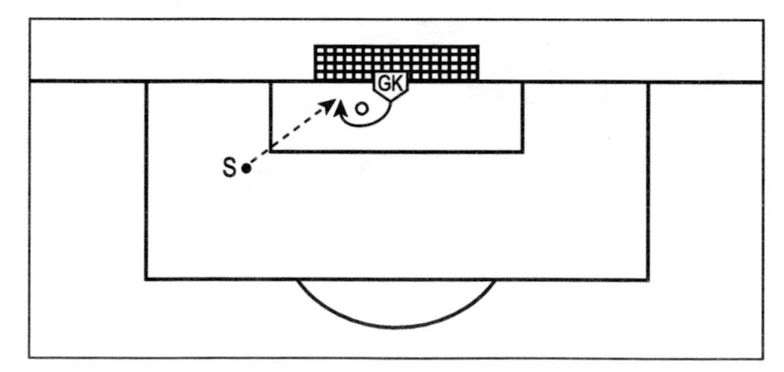

Figure 13-8

Strength/Fitness

Goalkeeper Lunges: The goalkeeper stands in a ready position. She lunges on a slight angle forward to her right side, and then brings her left foot back up to ready position (see Figures 13-9 and 13-10). Have her perform two sets of eight to each side, and rest as needed between each set.

Tuck Jumps: The goalkeeper stands with her legs together. She hops twice and then quickly explodes up, bringing her knees to her chest (see Figure 13-11). Have her perform two sets of 10 with a two-minute rest between each set.

Figure 13-9

Figure 13-10

Figure 13-11

FAR-POST SAVE

Equipment Needed: Nine balls

Key Coaching Points: The goalkeeper should land on her side and be sure her top hand is on top of the ball and her bottom hand is behind the ball. Stress the importance of letting the ball hit the ground first to cushion her fall and to use the ground as her third hand. Her bottom arm should come out and away from her body. After the ball, her shoulder—not her elbow—should hit the ground. She should keep her neck steady and straight. She should dive toward the ball at a forward angle and keep her bottom leg slightly bent and on the ground to maintain her balance on her side. When diving low, her bottom hand will have the best reach. Always use two hands when possible. If she cannot save the shot with two hands, insist that she use a flat palm to redirect the ball out of bounds. The number one rule of diving: *only dive when necessary*. Solid footwork should be stressed. Make sure the keeper is using the correct number of steps. This will vary depending on size and strength of the goalkeeper.

Warm-Up Activities

In the 18-yard box, randomly place four soccer balls. The goalkeepers jog around in all directions in the 18-yard box. On the coach's signal, they perform the following exercises. Have them perform each exercise twice. Stretch and rest as needed between each exercise.

- Sprint and touch each ball once, and then return to jogging.
- Quickly do three lateral jumps over each ball once, and then return to jogging.
- Quickly lay flat on their backs next to each ball once, and then return jogging.
- Perform a low dive on each ball once, and then return jogging.

□ Ball Gymnastics

Stretch and rest as needed between exercises.

Reverse Diving: One goalkeeper is standing with a ball in her hands. The other goalkeeper is lying on the ground on her side. The keeper with the ball tosses the ball up in the air so that the keeper on the ground can quickly get up and catch the ball before it hits the ground. As soon as the keeper with the ball tosses the ball in the air, she quickly dives on the ground, staying on her side as if low-diving to a ball. Make sure they alternate the side on which they dive down. They continue this exercise until each keeper has gone 10 times.

Hike: Each goalkeeper has a ball. Standing with her legs shoulder-width apart, she hikes the ball up between her legs so that the ball comes up and around her back and over her shoulder so she is able to catch the ball. Make sure she alternates the shoulder over which the ball goes. Have her perform one set of 12 repetitions.

Near, Far

Place a ball three yards out from the goal line and just inside the near post. The goalkeeper begins by performing a low dive on the stationary ball. Once she quickly gains her feet, the server, who is approximately 12 yards away, sends a firm ball just inside the far post (see Figure 14-1). Perform two sets of eight on each side of the goal.

Coaching Notes: After making her first save, the keeper should get up without using her hands. This ability will enable her to use her hands quickly for the shot. If she stays on her side and moves at game pace when diving for the first ball, she will have enough momentum to rock back on her legs and regain her ready position quickly. Have her practice this technique before you begin the exercise.

High Five

Goalkeeper one stands just inside the goalpost facing goalkeeper two. The server is 12 yards away. Goalkeeper one begins the exercise by doing a forward roll toward goalkeeper two. Once she is on her feet, she gives goalkeeper number two a high five (slap hands with each other). She then quickly turns to face the server. The server gives

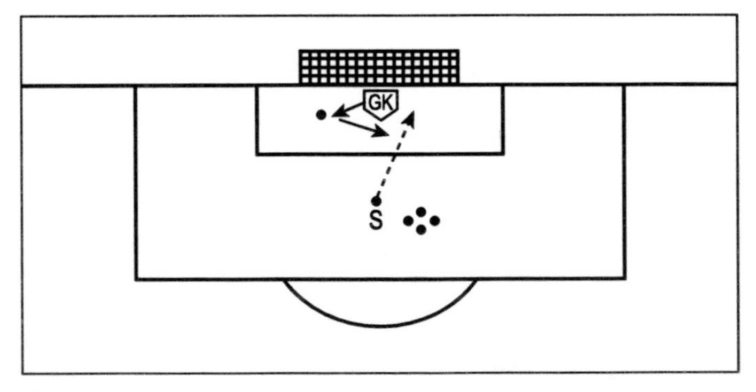

Figure 14-1

a firm ball just inside the far post. Goalkeeper one goes back to her starting position and then goalkeeper two begins the exercise (see Figure 14-2). Perform one set of eight, and then have the goalkeepers switch sides and perform a second set of eight.

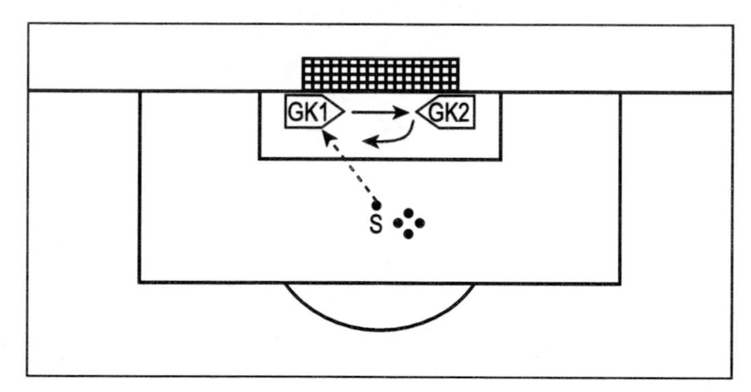

Figure 14-2

Strength/Fitness

AB Twist: The goalkeeper sits on the ground with her legs up and her knees slightly bent. Holding a ball with both hands, she quickly twists from side to side, bringing the ball down each time she twists to touch the ground (see Figure 14-3). Perform two sets of 30.

18-Yard Shuttle Run: Starting on the goal line, the goalkeepers sprint to the 18-yard line and back three times. Multiply the time it takes to perform one set by three and have them rest for that amount of time. Have them perform three sets.

Figure 14-3

MAKING THE SECOND SAVE

Equipment Needed: 10 balls

Key Coaching Points: The goalkeeper should land on her side and be sure her top hand is on top of the ball and her bottom hand is behind the ball. Stress the importance of letting the ball hit the ground first to cushion her fall and of using the ground as her third hand. Her bottom arm should come out and away from her body. After the ball, her shoulder—not her elbow—should hit the ground. She should keep her neck steady and straight. She should dive toward the ball at a forward angle and keep her bottom leg slightly bent and on the ground to maintain her balance on her side. When diving low, her bottom hand will have the best reach. Always use two hands when possible. If she cannot save the shot with two hands, insist that she use a flat palm to redirect the ball out of bounds. The number one rule of diving: *only dive when necessary*. Try to make the exercise as realistic as possible in relation to the amount of time between the first and second saves. Give enough time for your goalkeeper to have some success, but push her as much as possible.

Warm-Up Activities

Have the keepers perform each exercise for 30 seconds. Stretch and rest as needed between exercises.

The goalkeepers jog together and perform the following exercises:

- Toss a ball back and forth to each other.
- Roll a ball back and forth to each other.

The goalkeepers shuffle facing each other and perform the following exercises:

- Chest pass a ball back and forth to each other.
- Give a throw-in pass back and forth to each other.

- Ball Gymnastics

- The goalkeeper sits on the ground with legs straight and spread wide. She rolls the ball around her feet slowly five times in one direction, and then five more times in the opposite direction.
- The goalkeeper sits on the ground with legs straight and spread wide. She twists around and places the ball behind her back, and then twists in the opposite direction to retrieve the ball. Do five twists with the ball in both directions.

Light House

The server gives a below-the-waist toss to the goalkeeper. The goalkeeper performs a low dive. As soon as the goalkeeper makes the save, she quickly gives the server back the ball and regains her feet. The server continues this until the goalkeeper has completed a full circle (see Figure 15-1). Have them perform this exercise in both directions. Switch the goalkeeper between each set.

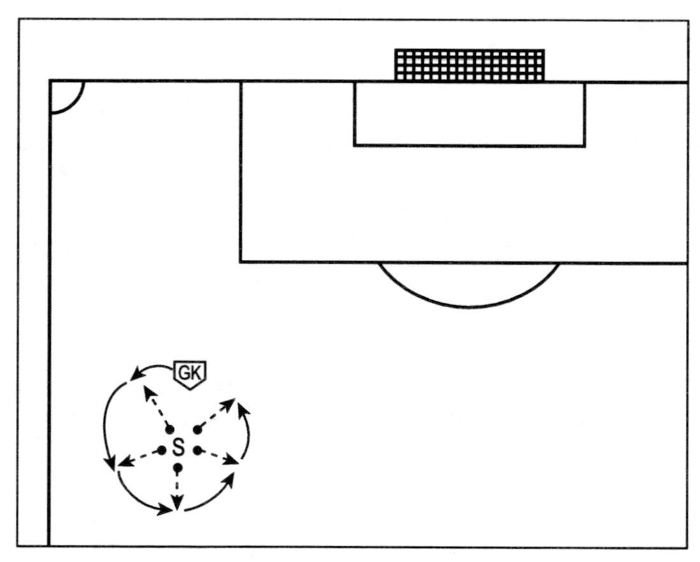

Figure 15-1

Second Save

Place ball 1 on the six-yard line and ball 2 on the penalty spot. Both goalkeepers stand side by side in the goal on the goal line. On the server's command, the working goalkeeper sprints out and dives down on ball 1. At the same time, the non-working goalkeeper runs to ball 2, turns, and shoots. As soon as the working goalkeeper makes the first save on ball 1, she quickly gains her feet to make the second save on ball 2 (see Figure 15-2). Have them perform two sets of eight. Switch the working goalkeeper after each set.

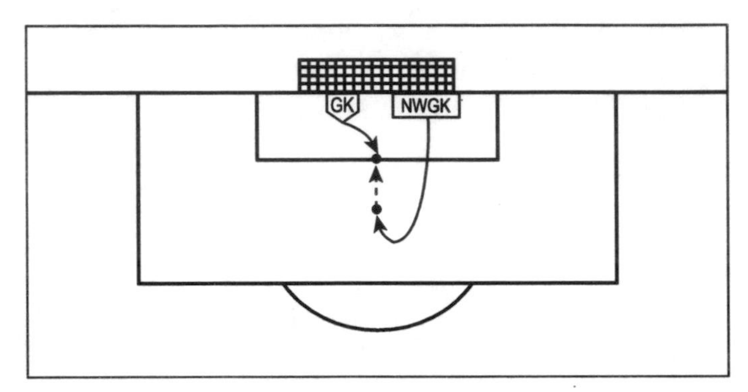

Figure 15-2

Strength/Fitness

10-for-10 Push-Ups: One goalkeeper performs 10 push-ups while the other goalkeeper rests. As soon as the first goalkeeper is finished, the second goalkeeper does 10 push-ups while the first goalkeeper rests. As soon as the second goalkeeper has performed 10 push-ups, the first goalkeeper performs nine push-ups, and after she is finished the second goalkeeper performs nine push-ups. They continue this process until the final set, which is one push-up each (for a total of 55 push-ups).

Split Jumps: Standing, the goalkeeper hops twice on both feet, then explodes up, splits her legs with one leg forward and one leg back, and then lands with both feet together. Have her perform two sets of 10 with a one-minute rest period between sets.

FORWARD DIVING

Equipment Needed: Eight cones and 10 balls

Key Coaching Points: This dive is most useful for low and hard shots—especially in wet conditions. Shoulders should be square to the ball. The goalkeeper should land on her forearms and keep legs flat once on the ground.

Warm-Up Activities

□ Footwork

Place eight cones in a row, one yard apart. Have the keepers perform three sets of each exercise. Stretch and rest as needed between exercises.

High Knees: To start, the goalkeeper faces the cones. At speed, the goalkeeper goes over each cone, bringing her knees up high. When she reaches the end of the row, she backpedals to the starting point

Slalom: To start, the goalkeeper faces the cones. Using a side-step slalom, she should go through all of the cones and then sprint back to the starting position.

In and Out: The goalkeeper starts with the left shoulder leading through the cones. With a slight bend in the knees, while balancing on the balls of her feet, the goalkeeper should weave in and out of the cones, keeping her hips square, head up, eyes forward, and hands ready (see Figure 5-1 in Session #5).

□ V-Sits

The goalkeeper sits on the ground with her legs out in front of her, as shown in Figures 13-2 and 13-3 in Session #13. The server gives an underhand toss to one side. The goalkeeper dives at a forward angle, trying to save the ball up toward her feet, creating a "V" when she saves the ball. *Coaching Notes: V-sits help goalkeepers warm up in two ways. First, they warm up her hands, shoulders, and neck, thus preparing her upper body for the task of diving. Second, they prepare her mentally to always attack the ball and dive toward the ball at a forward angle.*

□ Ball Gymnastics

Perform one set of 12 repetitions for each exercise. Stretch and rest as needed.

- The goalkeeper sits on the ground with her legs straight and off the ground and a ball between her feet to begin the exercise. She rolls the ball down from her feet to her chest, and then rocks forward to get the ball back up to her feet. Her feet should never touch the ground and she should not use her hands (see Figure 11-2 in Session #11).
- The goalkeeper sits on the ground with her legs up and spread, and a ball in her hands. Keeping her feet up, have her rotate the ball between her legs in a figure-eight pattern (see Figure 11-3 in Session #11).

Give and Get

Set up a small goal with two cones six yards apart. The goalkeepers stand on each side of the goal about six yards apart facing each other. Have the perform one set of six of each exercise.

- Place a ball on the goal line. Goalkeeper one performs a forward dive on the stationary ball. As soon as she makes the save, she leaves the ball on the line and quickly backpedals to her original starting position. As soon as goalkeeper one is up and away from the ball, goalkeeper two performs a forward dive. Repeat (see Figures 16-1 and 16-2).
- Goalkeeper one starts with the ball in her hands. She firmly bowls the ball at goalkeeper two, who performs a forward dive. Goalkeeper two keeps the ball and moves back to her starting position before she bowls the ball at goalkeeper one.
- Goalkeeper one starts with the ball in her hands. She firmly tosses a ball at the knees of goalkeeper two, who performs a forward dive. Goalkeeper two keeps the ball and moves back to her starting position before she tosses the ball at goalkeeper one (see Figure 16-3).

No Mercy

The goalkeeper begins in the goalmouth, three yards off the goal line. The server is 10 yards away. The non-working goalkeeper is standing off to the side facing the goalkeeper. The server shoots a hard shot right at the knees of the goalkeeper. The non-working goalkeeper follows the shot and may shoot or take the keeper on 1v1 if there is a rebound. After the goalkeeper performs the forward dive and makes the save, she quickly tosses the ball back to the server and prepares for the next shot (see Figure 16-4). Have them perform one set of eight repetitions.

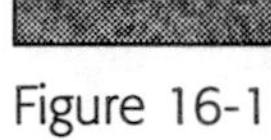

Figure 16-1

Figure 16-2

Figure 16-3

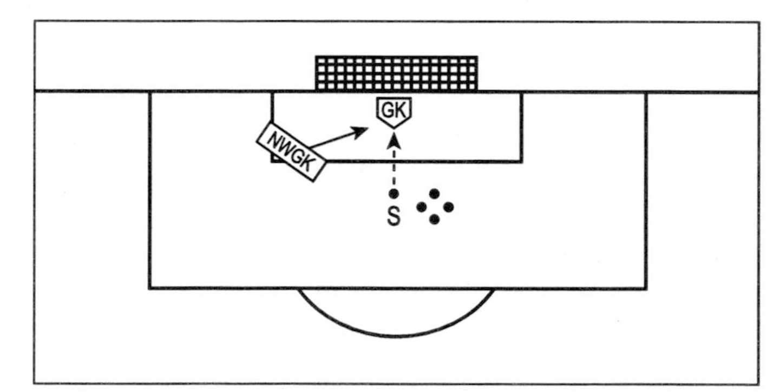

Figure 16-4

Strength/Fitness

Lat Raises: The working goalkeeper begins with her arms at her side. The non-working goalkeeper stands behind the keeper with her hands on the goalkeeper's arms right above her wrists. While the non-working goalkeeper provides resistance, the goalkeeper tries to bring her arms up until they are parallel with the ground. Once her arms are up, the non-working goalkeeper tries to push her arms back down while the goalkeeper resists enough to lower her arms slowly. Have them perform one set of eight repetitions.

Burppies: Both goalkeepers stand with their feet together. First, they throw their legs out behind them, forcing them into a push-up position. Second, they quickly bring their legs back in and return to a standing position. Have them perform one set of 10 repetitions.

COMBINATION

Equipment Needed: 12 balls and eight cones

Key Coaching Points: The goalkeeper should land on her side and be sure her top hand is on top of the ball and her bottom hand is behind the ball. Stress the importance of letting the ball hit the ground first to cushion her fall and of using the ground as her third hand. Her bottom arm should come out and away from her body. After the ball, her shoulder—not her elbow—should hit the ground. She should keep her neck steady and straight. She should dive toward the ball at a forward angle and keep her bottom leg slightly bent and on the ground to maintain her balance on her side. When diving low, her bottom hand will have the best reach. Always use two hands when possible. If she cannot save the shot with two hands, insist that she use a flat palm to redirect the ball out of bounds. The number one rule of diving: only dive when necessary. Solid footwork should be stressed. Make sure the keeper is using the correct number of steps. This number will vary depending on size and strength of the goalkeeper.

Warm-Up Activities

- Footwork

Place eight cones in a row one yard apart. Have the keepers perform each exercise three times up and back. Stretch as needed.

In and Out: The starting position is to the side of the cones. With a slight bend to the knees, while balancing on the balls of her feet, the goalkeeper should weave in and out of the cones, keeping her hips square, head up, eyes forward, and hands ready (see Figure 5-1 in Session #5).

Up and Over: The starting position is to the side of the cones. The leg nearest to the cone goes over first and then the second leg follows. With her knees coming up high, the goalkeeper should go up and over each cone, keeping her hips square, head up, eyes forward, and hands ready. Her feet should not touch or cross (see Figure 5-2 in Session #5).

Slalom: To start, the goalkeeper faces the cones. Using a side-step slalom, she should go through all of the cones and then sprint back to the starting position.

- V-Sits

The goalkeeper sits on the ground with her legs out in front of her, as shown in Figures 13-2 and 13-3 in Session #13. The server gives an underhand toss to one side. The goalkeeper dives at a forward angle, trying to save the ball up toward her feet, creating a "V" when she saves the ball. Have them perform one set of 12 repetitions. *Coaching Notes: V-sits help goalkeepers warm up in two ways. First, they warm up her hands, shoulders, and neck, thus preparing her upper body for the task of diving. Second, they prepare her mentally to always attack the ball and dive toward the ball at a forward angle.*

- Ball Gymnastics

Stretch as needed between each exercise.

Reverse Diving: One goalkeeper is standing with a ball in her hands. The other goalkeeper is lying on the ground on her side. The goalkeeper with the ball tosses the ball up in the air so that the goalkeeper on the ground can quickly get up and catch the ball before it hits the ground. As soon as the goalkeeper with the ball tosses the ball in the air, she quickly dives on the ground, staying on her side as if low-diving to a ball. Make sure they alternate the side on which they dive down. They continue this exercise until each goalkeeper has gone 10 times.

Hike: Each goalkeeper has a ball. Standing with her legs shoulder-width apart, she hikes the ball up between her legs so that the ball comes up and around her back and over her shoulder so she is able to catch the ball. Make sure she alternates the shoulder over which the ball goes. Have them perform one set of 12 repetitions.

Team Goalkeeping

Goalkeeper one stands five yards off the goal line and goalkeeper two stands three yards off the goal line. The server is 12 yards off the goal line with a supply of balls (see Figure 17-1). The server strikes a low shot, either toward the near post or far post. Goalkeeper one tries to save every shot taken. Any balls that get through goalkeeper one, goalkeeper two tries to save. For every goal scored, each goalkeeper has 10 push-ups. Have them perform two sets of 12 on each side of the goal. On the second and fourth sets, have goalkeepers change positions.

Near Post, Far Post

The goalkeeper begins the exercise standing in the middle of the goal on the goal line. When ready, she shuffles to the near post and pushes herself off the post, and quickly

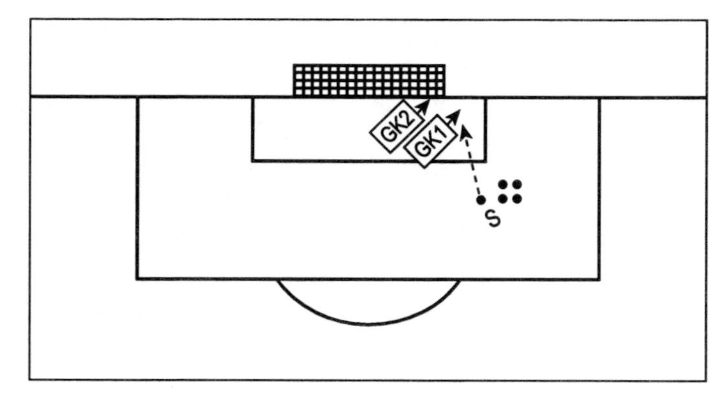

Figure 17-1

sets in ready position for a near post shot from the server. Soon after she makes the save and quickly regains her feet, the server drives a second shot toward the far post (see Figure 17-2). Have them perform two sets of eight on each side of the goal (every shot counts as one repetition).

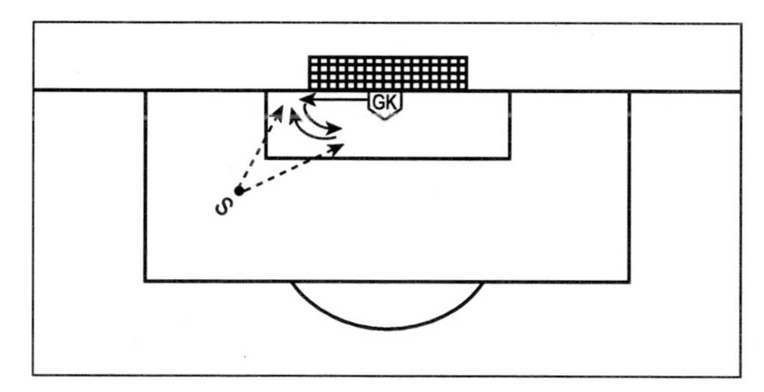

Figure 17-2

Strength/Fitness

Roll-Out Push-Ups: The goalkeeper starts out with her legs shoulder-width apart, her upper body bent down, and her hands on a ball midway between her feet. She rolls forward on the ball until her body is in a push-up position. She performs a push-up and then, without taking her hands off the ball or going down on her knees, she rolls back into the starting position (see Figure 2-6 in Session #2). Have her perform one set of 10.

Goalkeeper Lunges: The goalkeeper stands in a ready position. She lunges on a slight angle forward to her right side, and then brings her left foot back up to ready position (see Figures 13-9 and 13-10 in Session #13). Have her perform two sets of eight to each side. Rest as needed between each set.

5

1v1

SESSION #18

NO FEAR

Equipment Needed: Eight cones and eight balls

Key Coaching Points: The goalkeeper should approach the ball at the same pace at which the attacker is moving with the ball. The three opportunities to win the ball on a 1v1 are:

Smother—This approach can be used after the attacker touches the ball. The goalkeeper dives on the ball and covers it up. The smother is the easiest and safest way to win a 1v1.

Dive at the Attacker's Feet—As the attacker is shooting or just before the shot, the goalkeeper dives down and puts her hands on the ball. Insist that she dives hands first and stays on her side. This option is the most difficult and dangerous of the three.

Make a Wall—The goalkeeper quickly dives to the ground and makes herself as big as possible. Make sure her top arm is in front of her head to protect her face. The bottom leg should be bent slightly and on the ground to ensure balance. This technique should be used as a last resort.

Warm-Up Activities

- Footwork

Place eight cones or balls two feet to one yard apart. Have the keepers perform three sets of each exercise. Stretch and rest as needed.

In and Out: The starting position is to the side of the cones. With a slight bend in the knees, while balancing on the balls of the feet, the goalkeeper should weave in and out of the cones, keeping her hips square, head up, eyes forward, and hands ready (see Figure 5-1 in Session #5).

Up and Over: The starting position is to the side of the cones. The leg nearest to the cone goes over first and then the second leg follows. With her knees coming up high, the goalkeeper should go up and over each cone, keeping her hips square, head up, eyes forward, and hands ready. Her feet should not touch or cross each other (see Figure 5-2 in Session #5).

Extended In and Out: Move every other cone one yard up so the cones make a zigzag pattern. The technique is the same as described in the In and Out exercise, except her first step should be big. The leg closest to the cone should be used to take the first step. Her first step should beat the cone. Be sure the goalkeeper keeps her balance when backpedaling by staying low and keeping her weight on the balls of her feet (see Figure 7-2 in Session #7).

□ Square Work

Mark off a 12-by-12-yard grid. The server stands in the middle of the grid with a ball (place the rest of the balls just outside of the grid). Both goalkeepers move randomly in the grid. Have them perform one set of eight for each technique. When called on by the server, the goalkeepers perform one of the following:

- *Smother*: For the smother, the server randomly lays a ball on the ground.
- *Hands to the ball*: For hands to the ball, the server dribbles at the goalkeeper.
- *Wall*: For the wall, the server strikes a shot at the goalkeeper who is on the ground in the wall position.

□ Ball Gymnastics

Have the keepers perform one set of six repetitions of each exercise.

- The goalkeeper starts in a standing position, tosses the ball up in the air, performs a forward roll, and catches the ball above her head at the highest point possible.
- The goalkeeper begins in a sitting position. She tosses the ball up in the air and then quickly stands up to catch the ball above her head at the highest point. For greater challenge, have the goalkeeper try to stand up without using her hands.

Figure 18-1

Figure 18-2

No Fear

The goalkeeper begins the exercise up on her arms in a push-up position. The server stands on one side of her and the non-working goalkeeper stands on the other side of her. The server passes a medium-fast ball underneath the goalkeeper. As soon as the ball passes underneath, the goalkeeper quickly drops to her side to make a wall. The non-working goalkeeper strikes the ball into the goalkeeper (see Figures 18-1 and 18-2).

Goalkeeper vs. Goalkeeper

Place a second goal on top of the 18-yard box so that they face each other, or use cones to make two goals 18 yards apart. Put a ball midway between the two goals. One goalkeeper stands on each goal line. Alternating turns as the attacker, on the server's command, the attacker tries to dribble across the goalkeeper's goal line. For the second game, the attacker starts with the ball at her feet, but she must touch the ball three times before shooting. Play two five-minute games. *Coaching Notes: Make sure the goalkeeper approaches the ball at the same speed as the attacker. She should not wait for the attacker in her goal.*

Strength/Fitness

Manual Bench Press: The working goalkeeper lays flat on her back with a ball in her hands and her arms up and slightly bent. The other goalkeeper stands over her and puts pressure on the ball. The working goalkeeper resists (see Figure 1-4 in Session #1). Have them perform one set of eight at an eight-second count.

Leg Scissors: The goalkeeper sits on the ground with a ball. She raises her legs about six inches off the ground and leans backward slightly to find her balance. She then weaves the ball in and out of her legs. She should keep her legs as straight as possible (see Figure 1-5 in Session #1). Have her perform two sets of 25 repetitions.

STRONG HANDS

Equipment Needed: Eight balls

Key Coaching Points: The goalkeeper should approach the ball at the same pace at which the attacker is moving with the ball. The three opportunities to win the ball on a 1v1 are:

- Smother–This approach can be used after the attacker touches the ball. The goalkeeper dives on the ball and covers up. The smother is the easiest and safest way to win a 1v1.
- Diving at the Attacker's Feet–As the attacker is shooting or just before the shot, the goalkeeper dives down and puts her hands on the ball. Insist that she dives hands first and stays on her side. This option is the most difficult and dangerous of the three.
- Making a Wall–The goalkeeper quickly dives to the ground and makes herself as big as possible. Make sure her top arm is in front of her head to protect her face. The bottom leg should be bent slightly and on the ground to ensure balance. This technique should be used as a last resort

Warm-Up Activities

Using one ball, both goalkeepers jog around and perform the following exercises. Have them perform each exercise for 30 seconds. Rest and stretch as needed.

- Toss the ball back and forth to each other
- Bowl the ball back and forth to each other
- Bowl a ball out so the other goalkeeper has to perform a low dive
- Randomly toss a ball out so the other goalkeeper has to smother the ball

- ☐ Ball Gymnastics

- The goalkeeper stands with feet more than shoulder-width apart and weaves a ball on the ground in and out of her legs in a figure-eight pattern. Have her perform one set at a 20-second interval in each direction.
- The goalkeeper stands with feet shoulder-width apart. Bent over with both hands on the ball, she tosses the ball between her legs and then quickly moves her arms to the back of her legs to catch the ball before it hit the ground. Have her perform two sets of 12 repetitions.

- ☐ Low-Diving Circuit

Have the keepers perform one set of 12 for each exercise.

V-Sits: The goalkeeper sits on the ground with her legs out in front of her (see Figures 13-2 and 13-3 in Session #13). The server gives her an underhand toss to one side. The goalkeeper dives forward at an angle toward the ball, trying to save the ball up toward her feet, creating a "V" when she saves the ball. *Coaching Notes: V-sits help goalkeepers warm up in two ways. First, they warm up her hands, shoulders, and neck, thus preparing her upper body for the task of diving. Second, they prepare her mentally to always attack the ball and dive toward the ball at a forward angle.*

Kneeling: The goalkeeper kneels on the ground and the server strikes a ball at face or chest level. Serves should steadily increase in velocity (see Figure 13-4 in Session #13). *Coaching Notes: This exercise is great for improving hand and arm strength. The kneeling position forces the keeper to use her hands and arms, instead of relying on the balance and strength of her legs.*

Standing: From a standing position, the goalkeeper performs a low dive using one step (see Figures 13-5 through 13-7 in Session #13).

Hands to the Ball

Line up eight balls one to two feet apart. The goalkeeper begins in a sitting position next to, but slightly behind, the first ball. On the server's command, she dives down on the first ball just as the server is striking it. As soon as she stops the first ball, she pushes off with her legs to quickly get her hands on the next ball (see Figures 19-1 and 19-2). Have her perform two sets of eight on each side. *Coaching Notes: This exercise is great for teaching the importance of getting your hands to the ball and for building strength and confidence.*

Five-Second Drill

The goalkeeper begins the exercise on her goal line. The server and non-working goalkeeper are at the top of the 18-yard box with a supply of balls. On the server's

Figure 19-1

Figure 19-2

command, the non-working goalkeeper dribbles the ball at the goalkeeper. The goalkeeper comes off her line to defend the 1v1. The non-working goalkeeper has five seconds to dribble the ball across the goal line to score. She may not shoot the ball. The server counts the five seconds out loud. Once finished the server dribbles the ball and the non-working goalkeeper counts the five seconds. Have them perform two sets of eight.

Strength /Fitness

18-Yard Box Sprint Circuit: Following Figure 19-3, have the keepers perform the following circuit three times.

- Sprint 1, jog 2, 3, 4
- Sprint 1, 2, jog 3, 4
- Sprint 1, 2, 3, jog 4
- Sprint 1, 2, 3, 4

10-for-10 Push-Ups: One goalkeeper does 10 push-ups while the other rests. As soon as she has done her 10, the other goalkeeper does 10 push-ups. As soon as the second goalkeeper finishes her 10, the first goalkeeper does nine push-ups. Continue this process until each goalkeeper finishes the exercise by performing one push-up.

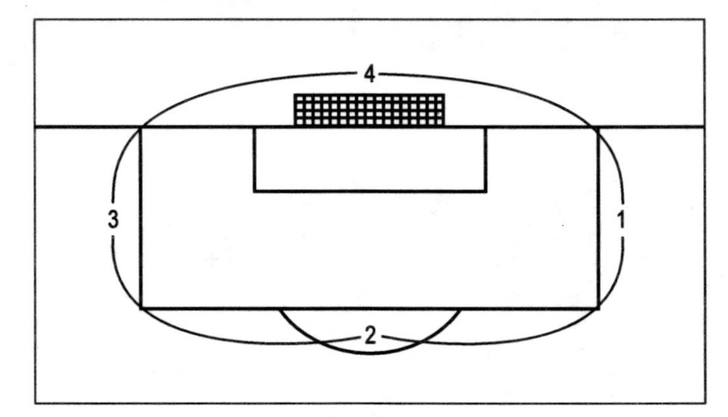

Figure 19-3

NARROWING THE ANGLE

Equipment Needed: Eight cones and six balls

Key Coaching Points: The goalkeeper should approach the ball at the same pace at which the attacker is moving with the ball. The three opportunities to win the ball on a 1v1 are:

- Smother–This approach can be used after the attacker touches the ball. The goalkeeper dives on the ball and covers up. The smother is the easiest and safest way to win a 1v1.
- Diving at the Attacker's Feet–As the attacker is shooting or just before the shot, the goalkeeper dives down and puts her hands on the ball. Insist that she dives hands first and stays on her side. This option is the most difficult and dangerous of the three.
- Making a Wall–The goalkeeper quickly dives to the ground and makes herself as big as possible. Make sure her top arm is in front of her head to protect her face. The bottom leg should be bent slightly and on the ground to ensure balance. This technique should be used as a last resort

Warm-Up Activities

□ Footwork

Place eight cones or balls two feet to one yard apart. Perform three sets of each exercise. Stretch and rest as needed.

In and Out: The starting position is to the side of the cones. With a slight bend in the knees, while balancing on the balls or the feet, the goalkeeper should weave in and out of the cones, keeping her hips square, head up, eyes forward, and hands ready (see Figure 5-1 in Session #5).

Up and Over: The starting position is to the side of the cones. The leg nearest to the cone goes over first and then the second leg follows. With her knees coming up high, the goalkeeper should go up and over each cone, keeping her hips square, head up, eyes forward, and hands ready. Her feet should not touch or cross each other(see Figure 5-2 in Session #5).

Power Step: The starting position is directly facing the line of cones, one step to the side. The leg nearest the cone power-steps forward on a slight angle through the cones. The trail leg should follow but never touch the other leg. After each power step through the cones, the goalkeeper should freeze for a second in the set position, meaning she is ready to react to a shot. Throughout the exercise, she should stay on the balls of her feet for balance, with her head up, eyes forward, knees slightly bent, and hands ready (see Figure 20-1).

Figure 20-1

Extended In and Out: Move every other cone one yard up so the cones make a zigzag pattern. The technique is the same as described in the In and Out exercise, except her first step should be big. The leg closest to the cone should be used to take the first step. Her first step should beat the cone. Be sure the goalkeeper keeps her balance when backpedaling (see Figure 7-2 in Session #7).

□ V-Sits

The goalkeeper sits on the ground with her legs out in front of her (see Figures 13-2 and 13-3 in Session #13). The server gives her an underhand toss to one side. The goalkeeper dives forward, trying to save the ball up toward her feet, creating a "V" when she saves the ball. Have her perform one set of 12. *Coaching Notes: V-sits help goalkeepers warm up in two ways. First, they warm up her hands, shoulders, and neck, thus preparing her upper body for the task of diving. Second, they prepare her mentally to always attack the ball and dive toward the ball at a forward angle.*

□ Drop

Each goalkeeper is jogging directly behind a ball. On the server's command, she drops down to the ball as quickly as possible. For the first set, have the goalkeeper put her hands on the ball, and for the second set, have her land so the ball is touching her mid-section to simulate the wall technique. Have her perform two sets of eight.

□ Ball Gymnastics

Under and Over: The two goalkeepers stand back to back, about two feet away from each other, with legs shoulder-width apart. One goalkeeper starts out with a ball. They both bend over and the one without the ball takes the ball through her legs from the other goalkeeper's hands. They then arch their backs and the goalkeeper without the ball takes the ball over her head from the other's hands. Have them perform two sets of 10. *Coaching Notes: Make sure the players keep their eyes on the ball, always use two hands, and take the ball from each other. On the second set, have them switch roles so the one who gave the ball bending over now gives the ball arching back.*

The Twist: The goalkeepers stand back to back with their legs shoulder-width apart. One has a ball in her hands. Keeping their feet planted, they turn to the same side and pass off the ball, then quickly turn to the other side, continuing to pass the ball off using two hands. Have them perform two sets of 10.

1v1 Goalkeeper Game

Mark off the six-yard line, the seven-yard line, and the eight-yard line with a cone (see Figure 20-2). The goalkeeper begins the exercise on her goal line. The non-working goalkeeper begins on the 12-yard line with a supply of balls. The non-working goalkeeper passes the ball to the six-yard line. As soon as the ball reaches the six-yard line, both the goalkeeper and the non-working goalkeeper can go for the ball. If the

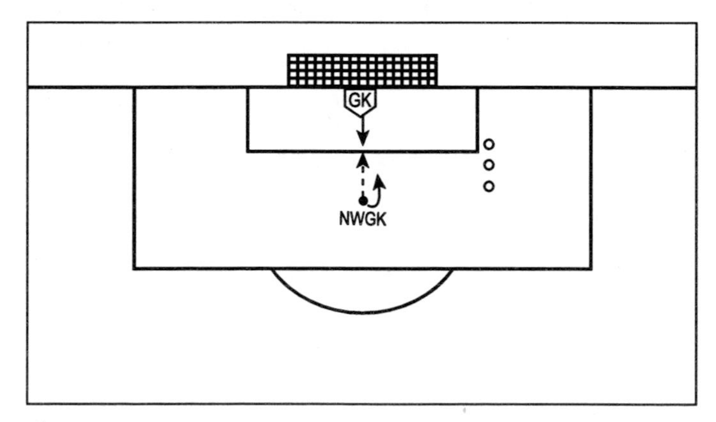

Figure 20-2

non-working goalkeeper reaches the ball first, she tries to beat the goalkeeper by dribbling the ball across the goal line. She may not shoot to score. Keep track of goals scored against each goalkeeper. The goalkeeper with the fewest goals against wins. Continue the exercise by passing the ball to the seven-yard line. Have them perform three sets of six (i.e., two passes to the six-yard line, two passes to the seven-yard line, and two passes to the eight-yard line).

Chase

Place two balls on the right-hand corner, the center, and the left-hand corner of the 18-yard box. The goalkeeper begins the exercise on the goal line. Starting at the right-hand corner, the non-working goalkeeper goes down on one knee five yards behind the server. When the server is ready, she begins to dribble at the goalkeeper. As soon as the server takes her first touch, the non-working goalkeeper gets up to defend and chases the server. The goalkeeper comes off her line to cut down the angle and defend the potential 1v1. Perform two sets of six. *Coaching Notes: Make sure the goalkeeper is helping the chasing defender by giving her good information (i.e., calling "Keeper" if she is going to go for the ball or telling the defender to force the attacker to the right or left).*

Strength /Fitness

Hand Slaps: The goalkeepers, with gloves off, face each other in a push-up position. On "Go," they each try to slap the other's hand. Their backs should stay straight and they should not go down on their knees (see Figure 3-5 in Session #3). Have them perform two sets at 20-second intervals. Give them at least 40 seconds rest between each set.

Goalkeeper Sit-Ups: The goalkeepers lay on their backs with feet touching. Using one ball, they take turns throwing the ball back and forth, doing a sit-up every time they catch the ball (see Figure 3-6 in Session #3). Have them perform two sets of 25.

SHOULD I STAY OR SHOULD I GO?

Equipment Needed: Four cones and 10 balls

Key Coaching Points: The goalkeeper should approach the ball at the same pace at which the attacker is moving with the ball. The three opportunities to win the ball on a 1v1 are:

- Smother–This approach can be used after the attacker touches the ball. The goalkeeper dives on the ball and covers up. The smother is the easiest and safest way to win a 1v1.
- Diving at the Attacker's Feet–As the attacker is shooting or just before the shot, the goalkeeper dives down and puts her hands on the ball. Insist that she dives hands first and stays on her side. This option is the most difficult and dangerous of the three.
- Making a Wall–The goalkeeper quickly dives to the ground and makes herself as big as possible. Make sure her top arm is in front of her head to protect her face. The bottom leg should be bent slightly and on the ground to ensure balance. This technique should be used as a last resort.

Warm-Up Activities

□ Square Work

Mark off a 12-by-12-yard grid. The server stands in the middle of the grid with a ball (place the rest of the balls just outside of the grid). Both goalkeepers move randomly in the grid. When called on by the server, the goalkeepers perform the following two exercises, two times each:

- Sprint and touch each cone in the grid.
- Dive down by each cone in the grid.

Next, when called on by the server, the goalkeepers perform one set of eight for each of the following techniques:

- *Smother*—The server randomly lays a ball on the ground.
- *Hands to the ball* (i.e., diving at the attacker's feet)—The server dribbles at the goalkeeper.
- *Wall save*—The server strikes a shot at the goalkeeper once the goalkeeper is in the wall position.

□ Ball Gymnastics

Under and Over: The two goalkeepers stand back to back, about two feet away from each other, with legs shoulder-width apart. One goalkeeper starts out with a ball. They both bend over and the one without the ball takes the ball through her legs from the other goalkeeper's hands. They then arch their backs, and the goalkeeper without the ball takes the ball over her head from the other's hands. Have them perform two sets of 10. *Coaching Notes: Make sure the players keep their eyes on the ball, always use two hands, and take the ball from each other. On the second set, have them switch roles so the one who gave the ball bending over now gives the ball arching back.*

The Twist: The goalkeepers stand back to back with their legs shoulder-width apart. One has a ball in her hands. They turn to the same side and pass off the ball, then quickly turn to the other side, continuing to pass the ball off using two hands. Have them perform two sets of 10.

Should I Stay or Should I Go?

The goalkeeper begins the exercise in the goalmouth. The server and non-working goalkeeper are at the top of the 18-yard box with a supply of balls. They pass the ball back and fourth to each other. Randomly, one of them takes a touch toward the goal and either takes a shot or dribbles in to take the goalkeeper on in a 1v1 situation. Have them perform two sets of 10. *Coaching Notes: Illustrate to your goalkeeper before the drill the visual cues an attacker gives before they shoot (i.e., looks up to find the goal and/or brings her leg back to shoot). Every time the goalkeeper thinks the attacker might shoot the ball, she must set in the ready position.*

1v1+1

The goalkeeper begins the exercise in the goalmouth. The server is at the top of the six-yard box with a ball, and the non-working goalkeeper is at the top of the 18-yard box. The server tosses a ball in the air for the goalkeeper to catch at the highest point. Right after the goalkeeper makes the save, she bowls the ball out to the non-working goalkeeper. The server then turns to defend against the non-working goalkeeper. The goalkeeper needs to communicate with her last defender and position herself correctly for a potential 1v1 situation. Defensive pressure should be about 50 to 70 percent to allow the goalkeeper the opportunity to practice a 1v1+1 situation. Have them perform two sets of 10.

Strength/ Fitness

Manual Bench Press: The working goalkeeper lays flat on her back with a ball in her hands and her arms up and slightly bent. The other goalkeeper stands over her and puts pressure on the ball. The working goalkeeper resists (see Figure 1-4 in Session #1). Have them perform one set of 10 at an eight-second count.

Leg Scissors: The goalkeeper sits on the ground with a ball. She raises her legs about six inches off the ground and leans backward slightly to find her balance. She then weaves the ball in and out of her legs. She should keep her legs as straight as possible (see Figure 1-5 in Session #1). Have her perform two sets of 25 repetitions.

6

Crosses

BELOW THE WAIST

Equipment Needed: 10 balls and eight cones

Key Coaching Points: The tuck technique is normally used when dealing with balls at waist height. Make sure the goalkeeper keeps her legs apart for balance. She should receive the ball with outstretched arms and cushion it by bending over. Her head should be over the ball, and her elbows as close together as possible. Insist that either the command "Keeper" or "Away" is used for every cross. To ensure balance and possession of the ball, the goalkeeper must go through the ball.

Warm-Up Activities

□ Footwork

Place eight balls or cones in a row, two to three feet apart. Have the keepers perform three sets of each exercise. Stretch as needed between exercises.

High Knees: The starting position is facing the cones. At speed, the goalkeeper goes over each cone, bringing her knees up high, and taking one quick step between each cone. Once at the end, she quickly backpedals to the starting point

Two-Leg Jump: The starting position is facing the cones. With legs together, the goalkeeper tries to jump up and over each cone. She should focus on the height of her jump and not how quickly she jumps over the cones.

*One-Leg Jum*p: The starting position is facing the cones. On one leg, the goalkeeper tries to jump as high as possible over each cone. Encourage her to use her arms and non-working leg to get as high as possible.

Pattern Jumping: The starting position is beside the first cone. With legs together, the goalkeeper jumps over the first cone, then up to the second cone, over the second cone, and up to the third cone, and so on.

- Ball Gymnastics

Stretch and rest as needed between each exercise.

Reverse Diving: One goalkeeper is standing with a ball in her hands. The other goalkeeper is lying on the ground on her side. The keeper with the ball tosses the ball up in the air so that the keeper on the ground can quickly get up and catch the ball before it hits the ground. As soon as the keeper with the ball tosses the ball in the air, she quickly dives on the ground, staying on her side as if low-diving to a ball. Make sure they alternate the side on which they dive down. They continue this exercise until each keeper has gone 10 times.

Hike: Each goalkeeper has a ball. Standing with her legs shoulder-width apart, she hikes the ball up between her legs so that the ball comes up and around her back and over her shoulder so she is able to catch the ball. Make sure she alternates the shoulder over which the ball goes. Have her perform one set of 12 repetitions.

Beat the Post

The goalkeeper begins in the back third of the goal facing the field and the server is just outside the 18-yard box right off the goal line (see Figure 22-1). The server kicks a firm cross on the ground toward the near post. The goalkeeper tries to collect the ball before it passes the near post. Have them perform two sets of 10 on each side of the goal. *Coaching Notes: Make sure your goalkeeper follows through the ball to maintain balance and possession of the ball.*

Near-Post Run

Use the same set up as in the previous exercise, except add the non-working goalkeeper as a near-post attacker. The server should vary the crosses from the ground to waist height. Have them perform two sets of 10 on each side of the goal. *Coaching*

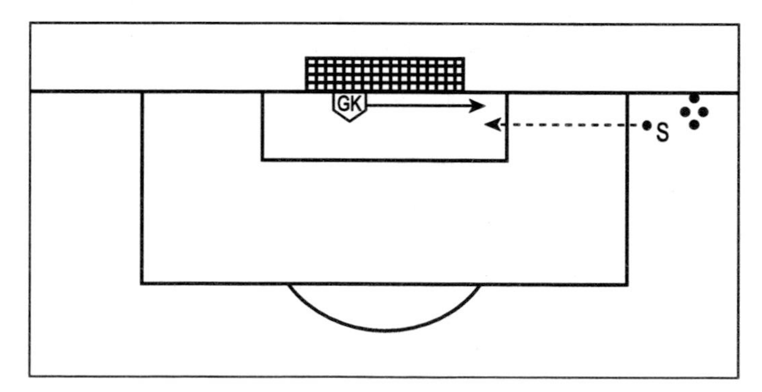

Figure 22-1

Notes: If the goalkeeper decides she needs to go down for the ball, make sure she goes all the way down into a forward dive or a low dive to ensure safe technique.

Strength/Fitness

Handstand: With support of the non-working goalkeeper, the goalkeeper performs a handstand for 20 seconds. Each goalkeeper should perform two handstands at 30-second intervals (see Figure 22-2).

Crossbar Taps: The goalkeeper begins inside the goalposts on the goal line. With outstretched arms, she tries to jump and touch the crossbar. Each goalkeeper should perform two sets of 10.

Figure 22-2

NEAR POST

Equipment Needed: Three cones and 10 balls

Key Coaching Points: Make sure she catches the ball at its highest point and practices going off one leg. The one-leg takeoff is similar to the lay-up technique in basketball. The hands should be behind and slightly underneath the ball.

Warm-Up Activities

Perform two sets of each exercise at 20-second intervals. Stretch and rest as needed.

- One goalkeeper lies on her back with her legs apart, about six inches off the ground. The other goalkeeper stands between her legs. The goalkeeper on the ground closes her legs, which will cause the standing goalkeeper to jump and spread her legs. The goalkeeper on the ground sets the rhythm for the standing goalkeeper (see Figure 23-1).

Figure 23-1

- Same situation as in the previous exercise, except the goalkeeper on the ground keeps her legs apart the whole time, while the standing goalkeeper quickly side steps (with high knees) in and out of her legs (see Figure 23-2).
- Same situation as in the previous exercise, except the standing goalkeeper does a two-leg hop in and out of the other goalkeeper's legs as quickly as possible (see Figure 23-3).
- Same situation as in the previous exercise, except the standing goalkeeper jumps in and out on one leg.

Figure 23-2

Figure 23-3

- ☐ Ball Gymnastics

- The goalkeeper sits on the ground with legs straight and spread wide. She rolls the ball around her feet slowly five times in one direction, and then five more times in the opposite direction.
- The goalkeeper sits on the ground with legs straight and spread wide. She twists around and places the ball behind her back, and then twists in the opposite direction to retrieve the ball. Have her perform five twists with the ball in both directions.

Highest Point

Place three cones in a triangle, approximately one yard apart. The goalkeeper begins at cone 1, the non-working goalkeeper stands at cone 2, and the server stands around three yards from the bottom of the triangle with a supply of balls. The server tosses a high ball over cone 2. The goalkeeper tries to catch the ball above the non-working goalkeeper's head at the highest point (see Figure 23-4). Have them perform three sets of 10. *Coaching Notes: Make sure she brings the leg closest to the attacking pressure in the high-knee position to help her protect herself, keep her balance when landing, and achieve maximum height in her jump. As the goalkeeper moves back to the starting position, the non-working goalkeeper shifts over to cone 3 and the exercise continues.*

Figure 23-4

Winning Near-Post Crosses

The goalkeeper begins halfway to two-thirds of the way back in her goal around two to three yards off her goal line. Place a cone four yards from the near post and four yards from the center of the goal line. The server is outside of the 18-yard box just off the goal line. The non-working goalkeeper stands on cone 1 (see Figure 23-5). The server drives a cross in the air suitable for a near-post run. Based on the height of the ball, the goalkeeper must then decide if she should win the cross in front of her attacker or behind her attacker. Have them perform two sets of eight on each side of the goal. On the second and fourth sets, have the non-working goalkeeper begin at cone 2 and allow her to move and challenge for the ball. *Coaching Notes: Have the goalkeeper use the attacker as a yardstick. If the attacker has no chance to win the ball with her head, the goalkeeper can win the ball behind her.*

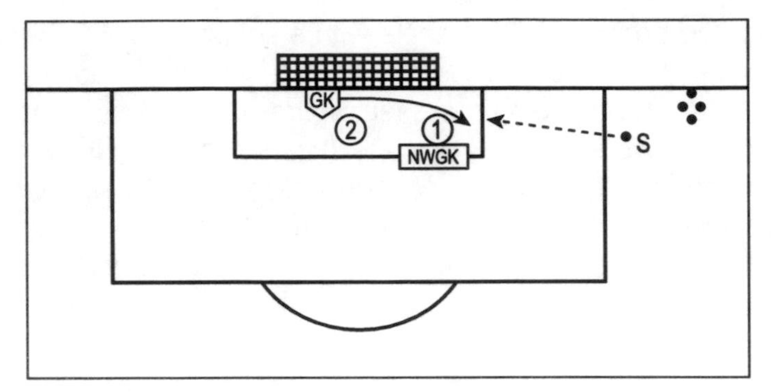

Figure 23-5

Strength/Fitness

Torso Lifts with a Ball: The goalkeeper lays flat on her stomach with a ball in her hands. She then lifts her torso off the ground and tries to lift the ball as high as possible. Have her perform two sets of 12.

One-Leg Calf Raise: Using the non-working goalkeeper for balance, the goalkeeper performs a one-leg calf raise. Have them perform two sets of 12 on each leg.

FAR POST

Equipment Needed: Two cones and 12 balls

Key Coaching Points: Make sure she catches the ball at its highest point and practices going off one leg. The one-leg takeoff is similar to the lay-up technique in basketball. The hands should be behind and slightly underneath the ball.

Warm-Up Activities

Have the keepers perform each exercise for one-minute intervals, stretch as needed.

- Both goalkeepers jog around in the 18-yard box, each with a ball. On command, each goalkeeper tosses a ball up to herself and, using the one-leg takeoff, catches the ball at the highest point.
- Same as the previous exercise, except now the goalkeepers toss a high ball to each other.

Have the keepers perform three sets at 20-second intervals for each exercise. Stop to stretch and rest as needed between sets.

- Each goalkeeper places her ball on the ground. On command, the keepers laterally jump over and back quickly on the balls of their feet.
- Same as the previous exercise, except now they jump to the front of the ball and then to the back.

□ Ball Gymnastics

Have the keepers perform one set of 12 repetitions for each exercise. Stretch and rest as needed.

- The goalkeeper sits on the ground with her feet up. She rolls the ball down from her feet to her chest, and then rocks forward to get the ball back up to her feet. Her feet should never touch the ground and she should not use her hands (see Figure 11-2 in Session #11).

- The goalkeeper sits on the ground with her legs up and spread, and a ball in her hands. Keeping her feet up, have her rotate the ball between her legs in a figure-eight pattern (see Figure 11-3 in Session #11).

Highest Point (Variation)

Have the keepers perform two sets of 12 of each exercise.

- The non-working goalkeeper stands stationary one yard in front of the goalkeeper. The server stands with a supply of balls two yards in front of the non-working goalkeeper. Alternating sides, the server tosses a ball high in the air just over the shoulder of the non-working goalkeeper. The goalkeeper, using the one-leg takeoff, catches the ball at the highest point.
- Same as the previous exercise, except the non-working goalkeeper can jump for the ball and try to head it away from the goalkeeper.

Winning Far-Post Crosses

The goalkeeper begins halfway to two-thirds of the way back in her goal around two to three yards off her goal line. Place a cone four yards from the far post and four yards from the center of the goal line. The server is outside of the 18-yard box just off the goal line. The non-working goalkeeper stands on cone 1 (see Figure 24-1). The server drives a cross in the air suitable for a far-post run. Based on the height of the ball, the goalkeeper must then decide if she should win the cross in front of her attacker or behind her attacker. Have them perform two sets of eight on each side of the goal. On the second and fourth sets, have the non-working goalkeeper begin at cone 2 and allow her to move and challenge for the ball. Coaching Notes: Have the goalkeeper use the attacker as a yardstick. If the attacker has no chance to win the ball with her head, the goalkeeper can win the ball behind her.

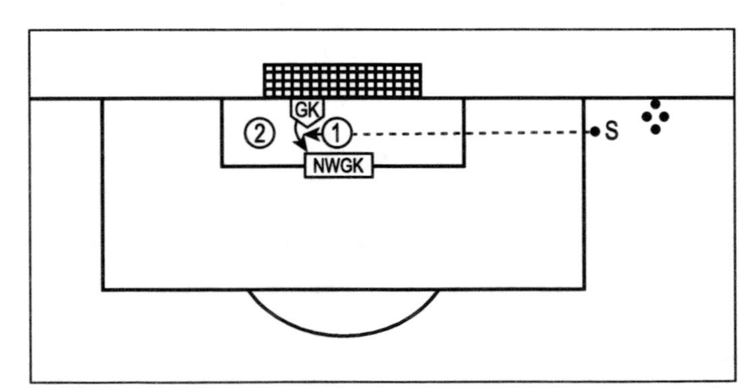

Figure 24-1

Strength/Fitness

Side to Side: The goalkeeper stands with legs apart slightly more than shoulder-width and hands behind her head. She shifts all of her weight to her right leg until her knee is in line with her toe, and then slowly shifts all of her weight to her left leg. At all times, she should be looking forward and have all of her weight on the heels of her feet (see Figures 24-2 and 24-3). Have her perform two sets at 30-second intervals.

Figure 24-2

Figure 24-3

Good Mornings: The goalkeeper stands with legs spread shoulder-width apart and hands behind her head. Always looking straight ahead, she slowly bends at the waist until her torso is parallel with the ground, and then slowly rises back up to the starting position (see Figures 24-4 and 24-5). Have her perform two sets of 12.

Figure 24-4

Figure 24-5

BEING AGGRESSIVE TOWARD THE BALL

Equipment Needed: Four cones and 10 balls

Key Coaching Points: Make sure she catches the ball at its highest point and practices going off one leg. The one-leg takeoff is similar to the lay-up technique in basketball. The hands should be behind and slightly underneath the ball.

Warm-Up Activities

Rest and stretch as needed.

□ Quick Feet

The exercise begins by both goalkeepers jogging in place. They listen for the following commands: shuffle right, shuffle left, or jump. After they quickly respond to a command, they return to jogging in place. Have them perform three sets of 30-second intervals.

□ Popcorn

Goalkeeper one lies on the ground in a push-up position. Goalkeeper two is one yard away with a ball in hand. Goalkeeper two tosses the ball straight up in the air and then quickly lies down in a push-up position. As soon as goalkeeper two tosses the ball in the air, goalkeeper one quickly gets to her feet and tries to catch the ball at the highest point. Have them perform two sets of eight repetitions.

□ Ball Gymnastics

Stretch as needed between each exercise.

Hike: Each goalkeeper has a ball. Standing with her legs shoulder-width apart, she hikes the ball up between her legs so that the ball comes up and around her back and over her shoulder so she is able to catch the ball. Make sure she alternates the shoulder over which the ball goes. Have her perform one set of 12 repetitions

Reverse Diving: One goalkeeper is standing with a ball in her hands. The other goalkeeper is lying on the ground on her side. The keeper with the ball tosses the ball up in the air so that the keeper on the ground can quickly get up and catch the ball before it hits the ground. As soon as the keeper with the ball tosses the ball in the air, she quickly dives on the ground, staying on her side as if low-diving to a ball. Make sure they alternate the side on which they dive down. They continue this exercise until each keeper has gone 10 times.

Side by Side

- The goalkeeper and the non-working goalkeeper sit side by side. The server stands two yards away from them with a supply of balls. The server tosses a ball up in the air so that it hangs between the two goalkeepers. The non-working goalkeeper tries to win the ball with her head by using her shoulder to push the goalkeeper out of the way. The goalkeeper tries to catch the ball at the highest point while fending off the non-working goalkeeper. Have them perform two sets of 12 for each goalkeeper (see Figure 25-1).
- In a 10-by-10-yard grid, both goalkeepers move around in all different directions. The server, who stands outside the grid, randomly tosses a ball up in the air. The goalkeeper fights to catch the ball at the highest point while the non-working goalkeeper tries to win the ball with her head. Keep track of which goalkeeper catches the most balls. At the end of eight servers, the goalkeepers switch roles. After each goalkeeper gets a turn, the keeper with the least amount of catches has 20 push-ups. Play this game twice.

Figure 25-1

Crossing Ladder

Place a cone four, six, and eight yards off the goal line (see Figure 25-2). The server is outside of the 18-yard box with a supply of balls. As the server dribbles down the flank, the goalkeeper moves accordingly to prepare for the cross. The server crosses the ball, varying the cross between the four-, six-, and eight-yard markers. Perform two sets of 10 on each side of the goal for both goalkeepers. For the second and fourth sets, have the non-working goalkeeper act as an attacker.

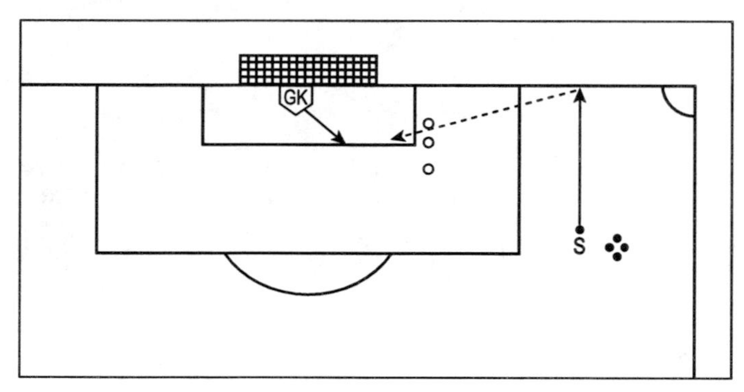

Figure 25-2

Strength/Fitness

Side Catch: The goalkeeper is balancing on her side. The non-working goalkeeper gives an underhand toss to the goalkeeper, who catches and tosses the ball back using only the one hand (see Figures 25-3 and 25-4). Have them perform two sets of 12 on each side.

Figure 25-3

Figure 25-4

Abdominal Ball Rolls: Both goalkeepers have a ball and are on their knees with the ball on the ground. Using both hands, they slowly roll the ball out until their torso and hips are parallel with the ground, and then slowly roll back to the starting position (see Figures 25-5 and 25-6). Have them perform one set of 12.

Figure 25-5

Figure 25-6

COMBINATION

Equipment Needed: Two cones and 12 balls

Key Coaching Points: Make sure she catches the ball at its highest point and practices going off one leg. The one-leg takeoff is similar to the lay-up technique in basketball. The hands should be behind and slightly underneath the ball.

Warm-Up Activities

Have the keepers perform each exercise for one minute. Rest and stretch as needed between exercises.

- Both goalkeepers jog around in the 18-yard box bouncing and catching a ball. On command, they drop their ball and run to the furthest line in the 18-yard box, and then back to their ball and continue jogging and bouncing the ball.
- Same as the previous exercise, except on command, they bowl their balls in the opposite direction of the other goalkeeper. Each goalkeeper runs to get the other goalkeeper's ball, and then continues jogging and bouncing the ball.

□ Popcorn

Goalkeeper one lies on the ground in a push-up position. Goalkeeper two is one yard away with a ball in hand. Goalkeeper two tosses the ball straight up in the air and then quickly lies down in a push-up position. As soon as goalkeeper two tosses the ball in the air, goalkeeper one quickly gets to her feet and tries to catch the ball at the highest point. Have them perform two sets of eight repetitions

□ V-Sits

The goalkeeper sits on the ground with her legs out in front of her. The server gives her an underhand toss to one side. The goalkeeper dives toward the ball on an angle, trying to save the ball up toward her feet, creating a "V" when she saves the ball (see Figures 13-2 and 13-3 in Session #13). Have them perform one set of 12. *Coaching Notes: V-*

Sits help goalkeepers warm up in two ways. First, they warm up her hands, shoulders, and neck, thus preparing her upper body for the task of diving. Second, they prepare her mentally to always attack the ball and dive toward the ball at a forward angle.

□ Ball Gymnastics

Perform one set of six repetitions of each exercise.

- The goalkeeper starts in a standing position, tosses the ball up in the air, performs a forward roll, and then catches the ball above her head at the highest point possible.
- The goalkeeper begins in a sitting position, tosses the ball up in the air, and then quickly stands up to catch the ball above her head at the highest point. For greater challenge, have the goalkeeper try to stand up without using her hands.

Crossing and Throwing

The goalkeeper begins the exercise in the center of the goalmouth, the non-working goalkeeper is standing behind a small goal 25 yards out and the server is outside the 18- yard box just off the goal line with a supply of balls (see Figure 26-1). The server drives a cross either high or low. Right after the goalkeeper makes the save, she quickly looks in the opposite direction from the server and throws the ball between the cones to the non-working goalkeeper. On the second set, the non-working goalkeeper hangs out at the top of the six-yard box and challenges for the ball, acting as an attacker. Continue to have the goalkeeper throw the ball between the cones. Have each goalkeeper perform two sets of 10 on each side of the goal.

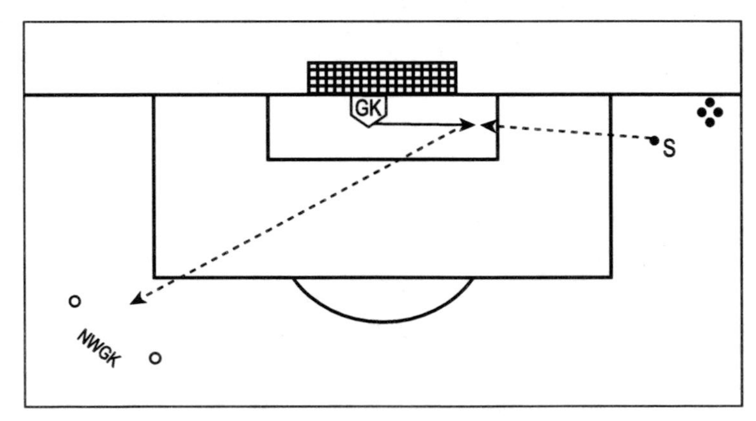

Figure 26-1

Crosses and Shot Stopping

The goalkeeper begins the exercise in the center of the goalmouth. The non-working goalkeeper is at the top of the 18-yard box with a supply of balls and the server is outside the 18-yard box about eight yards off the goal line with a supply of balls. Set a small goal 15 yards from the goal and off to the side (see Figure 26-2). The server crosses the ball, and after the goalkeeper makes the save, she quickly turns and bowls the ball toward the small goal. Right after the goalkeeper releases the ball, the non-working goalkeeper takes one touch to prepare the ball, and then drives a hard shot on goal. Have them perform one set of 10 on each side of the goal. Every serve counts as a repetition.

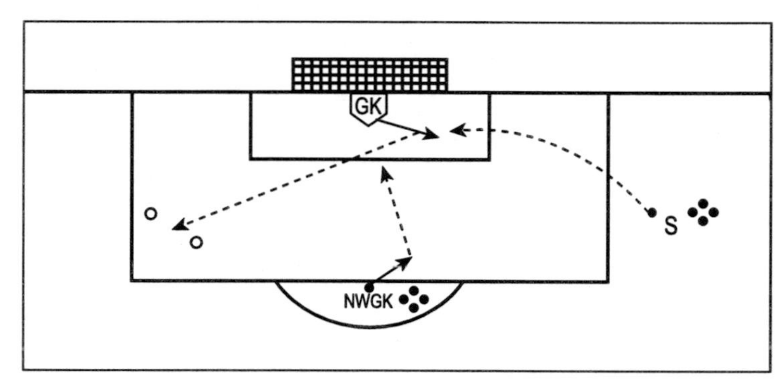

Figure 26-2

Strength/Fitness

Lower-Back Swimmers: Both goalkeepers lay flat on their stomachs with arms outstretched over their head. Lifting their torso and legs off the ground, they simulate a swimming motion by kicking their legs up and down simultaneous with their arms. Have them perform two sets at 20-second intervals.

Abdominal Rows: Both goalkeepers sit on the ground with legs together and knees bent. When ready, they lift and straighten their legs while they lean their torso back. Keeping their legs off the ground, they return back to the starting position and then repeat. Have them perform one set of 30.

7

Boxing

NEAR POST

Equipment Needed: Three cones and 10 balls

Key Coaching Points: When in doubt, box it out. This technique is best used when the weather is poor, when the shot or cross is too hard to handle, or when you have crowd of players with whom to contend. When possible, encourage your goalkeeper to box with two hands for best distance. Whether boxing with one hand or two, a flat surface is a must. To make that surface, have your goalkeeper place her thumb on top of her first finger. When using two hands, make sure her hands stay tight together when contact is made with the ball. When boxing near-post crosses, have her box the ball back where it came from; when boxing far-post crosses, have her box the ball in the direction it is moving. Encourage height, width, and length when boxing.

Warm-Up Activities

Have the keepers perform each exercise for one-minute intervals. Stretch and rest as needed.

- Both goalkeepers jog, skip, backpedal, and so forth around the 18-yard box.
- Same as the previous exercise, except add a ball to bounce and catch while moving.
- Have the goalkeepers move in all directions again in the 18-yard box, but roll a ball on the ground back and forth between each goalkeeper.

□ Boxing Circuit

The goalkeeper is sitting on the ground with legs spread in front of her. The server stands two yards in front of her with a ball. The non-working goalkeeper stands two yards behind the server. The server gives an underhand toss to the goalkeeper just above her head. Using two fists, the goalkeeper boxes the ball over the server to the non-working goalkeeper (see Figures 27-1 through 27-3). Have the keeper perform one set of 12 with two fists, then a set of 12 using the right fist only, and finish with a set of 12 using the left fist only.

Figure 27-1

Figure 27-2

Figure 27-3

□ Ball Gymnastics

Each goalkeeper has a ball. With legs spread slightly more than shoulder-width, each goalkeeper should try to catch the ball between her legs with one hand behind her legs and one hand in front of her legs. Have the keeper perform one set of 20 repetitions for each exercise.

- For the first set, have her bounce the ball between her legs and then quickly switch her hands to catch the ball between bounces (see Figure 27-4).
- For the second set challenge her not to let the ball hit the ground as she quickly switches her hands from front to back to catch the ball

Figure 27-4

Highest Point (Boxing Variation)

Place three cones in a triangle approximately one yard apart. The goalkeeper begins at the top of the triangle, the non-working goalkeeper stands next to cone 2, and the server stands around three yards from the bottom of the triangle with a supply of balls. The server tosses a high ball over cone 2. The goalkeeper tries to box the ball above the head of the non-working goalkeeper at the highest point (see Figure 27-5). Once the save is made, the goalkeeper returns to the starting position and the non-working goalkeeper quickly moves to cone 3. Have the keeper perform three sets of 10. *Coaching Notes: Make sure she brings the leg closest to the non-working goalkeeper in the high-knee position to help protect her, to keep her balance when landing, and to achieve maximum height in her jump. Encourage her to use two fists when possible.*

Figure 27-5

Boxing Near-Post Crosses

The goalkeeper begins halfway to two thirds of the way back in her goal, around two to three yards off her goal line. Place a cone four yards from the near post and four yards from the center of the goal line. The server is outside of the 18-yard box just off the goal line. The non-working goalkeeper stands on cone 1 (see Figure 27-6). The server drives a cross in the air suitable for a near-post runner to head the ball. Have the keepers perform two sets of eight on each side of the goal. On the second and fourth sets, have the non-working goalkeeper begin at cone 2 and allow her to move and challenge for the ball with her head. *Coaching Notes: When boxing near-post crosses, box the ball back where it came from. As with defensive headers, you want the ball to go high, wide and long.*

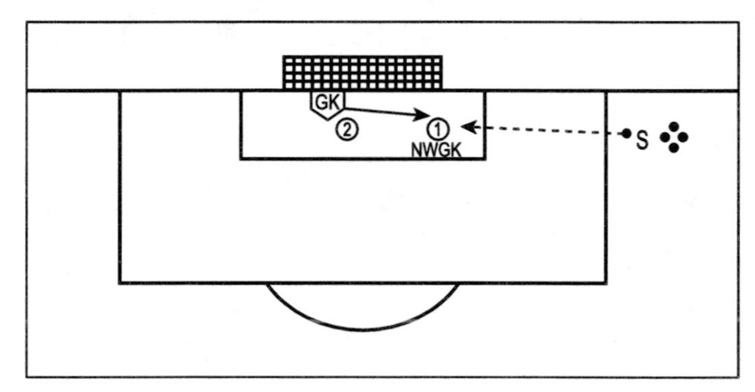

Figure 27-6

Strength/Fitness

Triceps Press on Bench: Using a team bench, have the keepers perform two sets of 10 triceps presses (see Figures 27-7 and 27-8).

Figure 27-7

Figure 27-8

Abdominal Toe Touches: The goalkeeper begins flat on her back with legs straight and arms above her head. Moving her arms and legs simultaneously, she touches her toes with her hands (see Figures 27-9 and 27-10). Have the keeper perform two sets of 12.

Figure 27-9

Figure 27-10

FAR POST

Equipment Needed: Eight cones and 12 balls

Key Coaching Points: When in doubt, box it out. This technique is best used when the weather is poor, when the shot or cross is too hard to handle, or when you have a crowd of players with whom to contend. When possible, encourage your goalkeeper to box with two hands for best distance. Whether boxing with one hand or two, a flat surface is a must. To make that surface, have your goalkeeper place her thumb on top of her first finger. When using two hands, make sure her hands stay tight together when contact is made with the ball. When boxing near-post crosses, have her box the ball back where it came from; when boxing far-post crosses, she should box the ball in the direction it is moving. Encourage height, width, and length when boxing.

Warm-Up Activities

□ Footwork

Place eight balls or cones in a row, two to three feet apart. Have the keeper perform three sets of each exercise. Stretch and rest as needed between exercises

High Knees: The starting position is facing the cones. At speed, the goalkeeper goes over each cone, bringing her knees up high, taking one quick step between each cone. Once at the end, she quickly backpedals to the starting point.

Two-Leg Jump: The starting position is facing the cones. With legs together, the goalkeeper jumps up and over each cone. She should focus on the height of her jump and not how quickly she jumps over the cones.

One-Leg Jump: The starting position is facing the cones. On one leg, the goalkeeper jumps as high as possible over each cone. Encourage her to use her arms and non-working leg to get as high as possible.

Pattern Jumping: The starting position is beside the first cone. With legs together, the goalkeeper jumps over the first cone, then up to the second cone, over the second cone, and up to the third cone, and so on.

□ Goalkeeper Juggling

The goalkeepers begin the exercise on the goal line. At their own pace, they box the ball with their fists above their heads. Have them juggle the ball this way to the top of the 18-yard box and back twice. *Coaching Note: Encourage them to use both hands together and separate. The higher they can box the ball into the air, the more difficult the exercise becomes.*

□ Ball Gymnastics

Under and Over: The two goalkeepers stand back to back, about two feet away from each other, with legs shoulder-width apart. One goalkeeper starts out with a ball. They both bend over, and the one without the ball takes the ball through her legs from the other goalkeeper's hands. They then arch their backs and the goalkeeper without the ball takes the ball over her head from the other's hands. Have the keepers perform two sets of 10. *Coaching Notes: Make sure the players keep their eyes on the ball, always use two hands, and take the ball from each other. On the second set, have them switch roles so the one who gave the ball bending over now gives the ball arching back.*

The Twist: The goalkeepers stand back to back with their legs shoulder-width apart. One has a ball in her hands. Keeping their feet planted, they turn to the same side and pass off the ball, then quickly turn to the other side, continuing to pass the ball off using two hands. Have the keepers perform two sets of 10.

Highest Point (For Boxing)

The goalkeeper begins one yard behind the non-working goalkeeper. The server stands around three yards from the non-working goalkeeper, with a supply of balls. The server tosses a high ball over the non-working goalkeeper. The goalkeeper tries to box the ball above the non-working goalkeeper's head at the highest point (see Figure 27-5 in Session #27). After the save is made, the goalkeeper returns to the starting position. Have the keeper perform two sets of 12. The first set use two fists, and the second set use one fist. Coaching Notes: Make sure she brings the leg closest to the non-working goalkeeper in the high-knee position to protect her, to help her keep her balance when landing, and to and achieve maximum height in her jump. To increase difficulty, have the non-working goalkeeper apply pressure by jumping and trying to head the ball.

Boxing Far-Post Crosses

The goalkeeper begins halfway to two thirds of the way back in her goal, around two to three yards off her goal line. Place a cone four yards from the far post and four yards from the center of the goal line. The server is outside of the 18-yard box just off the goal line. The non-working goalkeeper stands on cone 2 (see Figure 28-1). The server

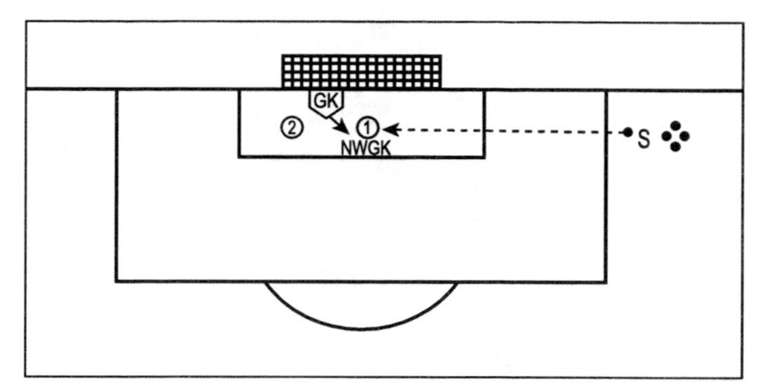

Figure 28-1

drives a cross in the air suitable for a far-post run. Based on the height of the ball, the goalkeeper must then decide if she should box the cross away in front of her attacker or behind her attacker. Have the keeper perform two sets of eight on each side of the goal. On the second and fourth sets, have the non-working goalkeeper begin at cone 3 and allow her to move and challenge for the ball. Coaching Notes: Have the goalkeeper use the attacker as a yardstick. If the attacker has no chance to win the ball with her head, the goalkeeper can win the ball behind her. When boxing far-post crosses, have the player box the ball in the direction that it is moving. Thus, if the ball was crossed from the right side and is headed for the left side, box the ball toward the left side. Encourage height, width, and length when boxing.

Strength/Fitness

Crunches: The goalkeeper lays flat on her back with legs up and bent at a 90-degree angle. With hands behind her head to support her neck, she brings her torso off the ground pointing her nose to the sky. Have the keeper perform two sets of 25.

Push-Ups on Fists: Have the keeper perform two sets of 12 push-ups on fists.

DEALING WITH A CROWD

Equipment Needed: Eight cones and 12 balls

Key Coaching Points: When in doubt, box it out. This technique is best used when the weather is poor, when the shot or cross is too hard to handle, or when you have a crowd of players with whom to contend. When possible, encourage your goalkeeper to box with two hands for best distance. Whether boxing with one hand or two, a flat surface is a must. To make that surface, have your goalkeeper place her thumb on top of her first finger. When using two hands, make sure her hands stay tight together when contact is made with the ball. When boxing near-post crosses, the keeper should box the ball back where it came from; when boxing far-post crosses, she should box the ball in the direction it is moving. Encourage height, width, and length when boxing.

Warm-Up Activities

- Footwork

Place eight cones or balls two feet to one yard apart. Have the keeper perform three sets of each exercise. Stretch and rest as needed.

In and Out: The starting position is to the side of the cones. With a slight bend in the knees, while balancing on the balls of the feet, the goalkeeper should weave in and out of the cones, keeping her hips square, head up, eyes forward, and hands ready (see Figure 5-1 in Session #5).

Up and Over: The starting position is to the side of the cones. The leg nearest to the cone goes over first and then the second leg follows. With her knees coming up high, the goalkeeper should go up and over each cone, keeping her hips square, head up, eyes forward, and hands ready. Her feet should not touch or cross each other (see Figure 5-2 in Session #5).

Lateral Hops: The starting position is to the side of the cones. Jumping with both legs together, the goalkeeper hops over each cone.

Extended In and Out: Move every other cone one yard up so the cones make a zigzag pattern. The technique is the same as described in the In and Out exercise, except her first step should be big. The leg closest to the cone should be used to take the first step. Her first step should beat the cone. Be sure the goalkeeper keeps her balance when backpedaling by staying low and keeping her weight on the balls of her feet (see Figure 7-2 in Session #7).

□ Goalkeeper (Juggling Variation)

Using the pattern short-short-long, each goalkeeper tries to box the ball above her head with two short boxes, and then a long box, which should be as high as possible. Have the keeper perform two sets at 30-second intervals, using two fists for the first set and one fist for the second set (alternating right and left).

□ Ball Gymnastics

Stretch and rest as needed.

- The goalkeeper stands with feet more than shoulder-width apart and weaves a ball on the ground in and out of her legs in a figure-eight pattern. Have the keeper perform two sets at 20-second intervals. On the second set, switch directions.
- The goalkeeper stands with feet shoulder-width apart. Bent over with both hands on the ball, she tosses the ball between her legs, and then quickly moves her arms to the back of her legs to catch the ball before it hits the ground. Have the keeper perform two sets of 12 repetitions.

Cone Jungle

Spread five cones in the goalmouth (as illustrated in Figure 29-1). The goalkeeper begins one third of the way to halfway back in her goal. The server is outside the 18-yard box, one to two yards off the goal line, with a supply of balls. The server crosses

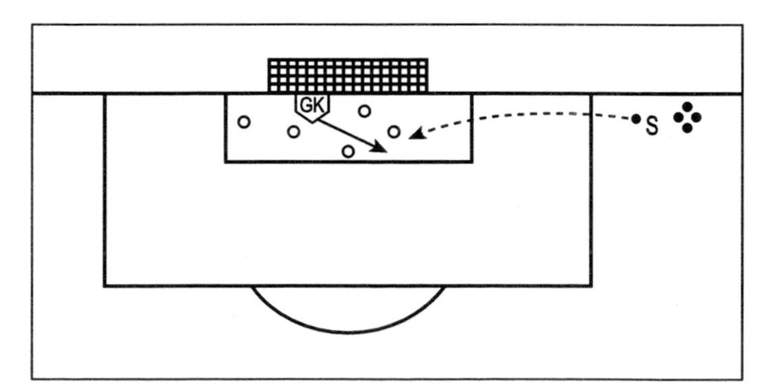

Figure 29-1

the ball in the air over the cones. The goalkeeper must box the ball away at the highest point without stepping on a cone. Have the keeper perform two sets of 10 on each side. On the second and fourth sets, have the non-working goalkeeper also challenge for the ball in addition to having the goalkeeper avoid stepping on the cones.

Fists of Fury

Both goalkeepers are in goal. The server is outside the 18-yard box, one to two yards off the goal line, with a supply of balls. The server crosses a ball in the air varying both far and near post. Both goalkeepers try to box the ball away. Every time a goalkeeper wins the ball, she gets a point. The goalkeeper with the most points at the end of 12 serves wins the game. The losing goalkeeper does 15 push-ups on her fists. Play two games, one on each side of the goal.

Strength/Fitness

Seals: The goalkeeper lays flat on her stomach with legs together and hands folded behind her back. Simultaneously she raises her torso and legs up off the ground, holds for two seconds, and then lowers her back to the starting position. Have the keeper perform two sets of 12.

One-Leg Squats: The goalkeeper begins the exercise with her right leg forward. She squats down until her left knee just barely touches the ground, then pushes up with the right leg to the starting position. Have the keeper perform two sets of 12 on each leg.

MAKING THE SECOND SAVE

Equipment Needed: 12 balls

Key Coaching Points: When in doubt, box it out. This technique is best used when the weather is poor, when the shot or cross is too hard to handle, or when you have a crowd of players with whom to contend. When possible, encourage your goalkeeper to box with two hands for best distance. Whether boxing with one hand or two, a flat surface is a must. To make that surface, have your goalkeeper place her thumb on top of her first finger. When using two hands, make sure her hands stay tight together when contact is made with the ball. When boxing near-post crosses, box the ball back where it came from; when boxing far-post crosses, box the ball in the direction it is moving. Encourage height, width, and length when boxing.

Warm-Up Activities

Both goalkeepers are in the 18-yard box moving around (i.e., skipping, jogging, and shuffling) at their own pace. After two minutes, have them stretch.

- V-Sits

The goalkeeper sits on the ground with her legs out in front of her. The server gives her an underhand toss to one side. The goalkeeper dives toward the ball on an angle, trying to save the ball up toward her feet, creating a "V" when she saves the ball (see Figures 13-2 and 13-3 in Session #13). Have the keeper perform one set of 12. *Coaching Notes: V-sits help goalkeepers warm up in two ways. First, they warm up her hands, shoulders, and neck, thus preparing her upper body for the task of diving. Second, they prepare her mentally to always attack the ball and dive toward the ball at a forward angle.*

- Boxing Circuit

The goalkeeper is sitting on the ground with legs spread in front of her. The server stands two yards in front of her with a ball. The non-working goalkeeper stands two yards behind the server. The server gives an underhand toss to the goalkeeper just above her head. The goalkeeper, using two fists, boxes the ball over the server to the non-working goalkeeper. Have the keeper perform one set of 12 with two fists, then a set of 12 using the right fist only, and finish with a set of 12 using the left fist only (see Figures 27-1 through 27-3 in Session #27).

□ Ball Gymnastics

Have the keepers perform two sets of 12 of each exercise. Rest and stretch as needed between sets.

- Each goalkeeper has a ball. She tosses the ball straight up above her head and then catches the ball behind her back. *Coaching Notes: Challenge them to throw the ball higher and higher. The trick to catching the ball behind the back is not to bend over.*
- Each goalkeeper has a ball. She holds the ball above and behind her head. She drops the ball and then quickly bends down to catch the ball by reaching between her legs.

Near-Post Box and Shot

The goalkeeper begins the exercise one third of the way to halfway back in the goal, one to two yards off the goal line. The server is outside of the 18-yard box, one to two yards off the goal line, with a supply of balls. The non-working goalkeeper is just outside of the 18-yard box, with a supply of balls (see Figure 30-1). The server sends a near-post cross in the air. As soon as the goalkeeper boxes the ball away, the non-working goalkeeper strikes a low shot on goal. Have the keeper perform two sets of 12 on each side of the goal. Every serve counts as one repetition.

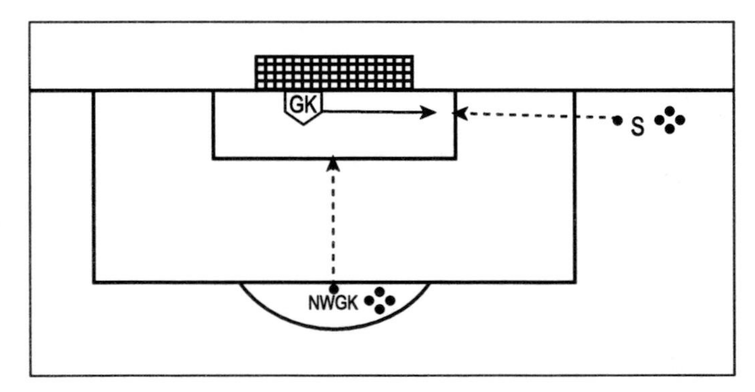

Figure 30-1

Far-Post Box and Shot

The goalkeeper begins the exercise one third of the way to halfway back in the goal, one to two yards off the goal line. The server is outside of the 18-yard box, one to two yards off the goal line, with a supply of balls. The non-working goalkeeper is on the other side of the 18-yard box, with a supply of balls (see Figure 30-1). Use the same set up as in the previous exercise, except the server sends a far post cross in the air. As soon as the goalkeeper boxes the ball away, the non-working goalkeeper strikes a low, hard shot. Have the keeper perform two sets of 12 on each side of the goal. Every serve counts as one repetition.

Strength/Fitness

Elevator Leg Lifts: Both goalkeepers lay flat on their backs with their hands under their lower backs for support. For 30-second intervals, they follow the following commands:

- "One" – both legs just off the ground
- "Two" – both legs one foot off the ground
- "Three" – both legs two feet off the ground

Legs should always stay straight and not touch the ground once the 30-second count has started. Have the keeper perform two sets at 30-second intervals.

Crab Walk Race: Both goalkeepers get into the crab position and race each other from the goal line to the top of the 18-yard box and back. The loser does 10 push-ups. Race twice.

COMBINATION

Equipment Needed: Two cones and 12 balls

Key Coaching Points: When in doubt, box it out. This technique is best used when the weather is poor, when the shot or cross is too hard to handle, or when you have a crowd of players with whom to contend. When possible, encourage your goalkeeper to box with two hands for best distance. Whether boxing with one hand or two, a flat surface is a must. To make that surface, have your goalkeeper place her thumb on top of her first finger. When using two hands, make sure her hands stay tight together when contact is made with the ball. When boxing near-post crosses, box the ball back where it came from; when boxing far-post crosses, box the ball in the direction it is moving. Encourage height, width, and length when boxing.

Warm-Up Activities

Rest and stretch as needed between exercises.

- Both goalkeepers stand in front of a ball. When ready, they quickly alternate their feet, tapping their foot on top of the ball. Have the keeper perform three sets at 20-second intervals.
- The goalkeeper begins in a sit-up position. The server stands a yard away and the non-working goalkeeper stands a yard behind the server. The server tosses a ball in the air and the goalkeeper performs a sit-up as she comes up to box the ball over the server's head to the non-working goalkeeper. Have the keeper perform two sets of 12. Use two fists for the first set, and alternate right and left fist for the second set.

□ V-Sits

The goalkeeper sits on the ground with her legs out in front of her. The server gives her an underhand toss to one side. The goalkeeper dives toward the ball on an angle, trying to save the ball up toward her feet, creating a "V" when she saves the ball (see Figures 13-2 and 13-3 in Session #13). Have the keeper perform one set of 12.

Coaching Notes: V-sits help goalkeepers warm up in two ways. First, they warm up her hands, shoulders, and neck, thus preparing her upper body for the task of diving. Second, they prepare her mentally to always attack the ball and dive toward the ball at a forward angle.

□ Ball Gymnastic

Stretch as needed between each exercise.

- The goalkeeper stands with a ball in her hands and her legs more than shoulder-width apart. In a figure-eight pattern, she weaves the ball at knee height between her legs. Have the keeper perform two sets at 20-second intervals and rest for 20-40 seconds between sets.
- The goalkeeper stands with a ball in her hands and her legs shoulder-width apart. The keeper bounces the ball between her legs, and then quickly moves her hands to catch the ball behind her. Have the keeper perform two sets of 10.

Near-Post Dive and Box

Place a ball just inside the near post and one yard off the goal line. The goalkeeper begins the exercise two yards away from the ball. The non-working goalkeeper stands in the goalmouth, and the server is outside of the 18-yard box, with a supply of balls (see Figure 31-1). The exercise begins by the goalkeeper diving on the stationary ball. As soon as she gains her feet, the server sends a near-post cross in the air for her to box away. Have the keeper perform two sets of eight on each side of the goal. On the first and third sets, the non-working goalkeeper is passive. On the second and fourth sets, the non-working goalkeeper makes a near-post run and tries to win the ball with her head.

Throw and Box

Place a small five-yard goal 25 yards out from the goal. The non-working goalkeeper is at penalty spot with a supply of balls, and the server is outside the 18-yard box with a

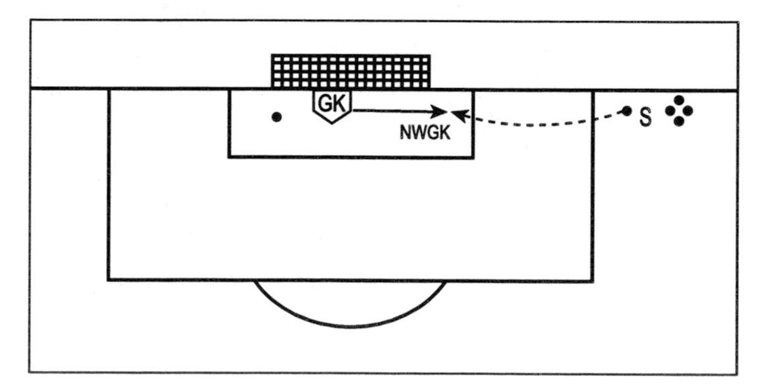

Figure 31-1

supply of balls (see Figure 31-2). The exercise begins with the non-working goalkeeper shooting a ball at the goalkeeper's hands. The goalkeeper performs an overhand throw through the small goal. Soon after the throw, the server drives a far-post cross in the air for the goalkeeper to box. Have the keeper perform two sets of 12 on each side of the goal. Every serve counts as one repetition. On the second and fourth sets, have the non-working goalkeeper make a far-post run and try to win the ball with her head.

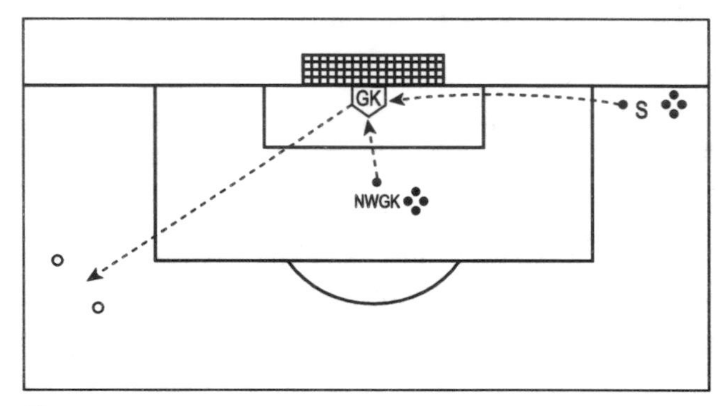

Figure 31-2

Strength/Fitness

Resistance Sprints: The non-working goalkeeper stands behind the goalkeeper, puts her hands on the goalkeeper's hips, and grabs a tight hold of her shorts. The goalkeeper sprints as fast as possible from the goal line to the 18-yard line. Encourage the goalkeeper to really drive her knees (see Figure 31-3). Once at the top of the 18-yard box, both goalkeepers walk back to the starting position. Have the keeper perform one set of five.

Figure 31-3

Wide Stance Push-Ups: Both goalkeepers are in a push-up position with their legs spread more than shoulder-width. Have the keeper perform one set of 12 push-ups.

8

Power Diving

SESSION #32

TRAINING THE TOP HAND

Equipment Needed: Eight cones and 10 balls

Key Coaching Points: The keeper should land on her side and be sure her top hand is on top of the ball, and her bottom hand is behind the ball. Stress the importance of letting the ball hit the ground first to cushion her fall, and of using the ground as her third hand. Her bottom arm should come out and away from her body. After the ball, her shoulder—not her elbow—should hit the ground. She should keep her neck steady and straight. She should dive toward the ball at a forward angle and keep her bottom leg slightly bent once on the ground to maintain her balance on her side. The goalkeeper's top hand will have the best reach when power-diving. Always use two hands when possible. If she cannot save the shot with two hands, insist that she use a flat palm to redirect the ball out of bounds. The number-one rule of diving: only dive when necessary. Power-diving is also referred to as "high diving" or "extension diving."

Warm-Up Activities

- Footwork

Place eight cones or balls two to three feet apart. Have the keeper perform three repetitions of each exercise. Stretch as needed between exercises.

In and Out: The starting position is to the side of the cones. With a slight bend in the knees, while balancing on the balls of the feet, the goalkeeper should weave in and out of the cones, keeping her hips square, head up, eyes forward, and hands ready (see Figure 5-1 in Session #5).

Up and Over: The starting position is to the side of the cones. The leg nearest to the cone goes over first and then the second leg follows. With her knees coming up high, the goalkeeper should go up and over each cone, keeping her hips square, head up, eyes forward and hands ready. Her feet should not touch or cross (see Figure 5-2 in Session #5).

Power Step: The starting position is directly facing the line of cones, one step to the side. The leg nearest the cone power-steps forward on a slight angle through the cones.

The trail leg should follow—but never touch—the other leg. After each power step through the cones, the goalkeeper should freeze for a second in the set position—meaning she is ready to react to a shot. Throughout the exercise, she should stay on the balls of her feet for balance, with her head up, eyes forward, knees slightly bent, and hands ready (see Figure 20-1 in Session #20).

□ V-Sits

The goalkeeper sits on the ground with her legs out in front of her. The server delivers an underhand toss to one side. The goalkeeper dives forward, trying to save the ball up toward her feet, thus creating a "V" when she saves the ball (see Figures 13-2 and 13-3 in Session #13). Have the keeper perform one set of 12. *Coaching Notes: V-sits help goalkeepers warm up in two ways. First, they warm up her hands, shoulders, and neck, thus preparing her upper body for the task of diving. Second, they prepare her mentally to always attack the ball and dive toward the ball at a forward angle.*

□ Ball Gymnastics

Perform one set of six repetitions of each exercise.

- The goalkeeper starts in a standing position, tosses the ball up in the air, performs a forward roll, and then catches the ball above her head at the highest point possible.
- The goalkeeper begins in a sitting position, tosses the ball up in the air, and then quickly stands up to catch the ball above her head at the highest point. For greater challenge, have her try to stand up without using her hands.

Top Hand

Place two cones 15 yards apart. The working goalkeeper begins on her knees next to the first cone. The server stands in front of the goalkeeper, about a yard away. Using an underhand toss, the server delivers the ball just to the outside of the goalkeeper. The goalkeeper can only use her top hand opposite from the ball to pin the ball to the ground (see Figures 32-1 and 32-2). The server/goalkeeper should repeat the toss/dive, moving closer to the second cone with each repetition. When they reach the second cone, they turn around and repeat, moving back to the first cone. Have the goalkeeper switch hands on the way back. Perform two sets. *Coaching Notes: Make sure her top hand is on top of the ball. As with all diving exercises, encourage her to dive at an angle toward the ball. You will know she is doing this technique correctly if she is moving at an angle away from the cones.*

Touch and Go

The goalkeeper starts in the middle of the goal. On the server's command, she shuffles to the right goalpost, touches the post, and then moves back toward the middle of the

Figure 32-1

Figure 32-2

goal. Once the goalkeeper is about in the middle of the goal, the server tosses an underhand shot shoulder height to the goalkeeper's left side. The goalkeeper performs a power dive. Alternate the starting goalpost for each repetition (see Figure 32-3). Have the keeper perform two sets of 10 repetitions. *Coaching Notes: Stress the use of the top hand. The ball should be the first thing to hit the ground to cushion the fall.*

Strength/Fitness

Free Fall: In a standing position, the goalkeeper tries to keep her body as straight as possible while she falls forward and catches herself on the ground. Challenge her not to put her arms out until the last minute. Have her perform two sets of eight repetitions.

Standing Broad Jump: The goalkeeper starts at the goal line. With feet shoulder-width apart, she bends her knees and jumps forward with both feet. Encourage her to use her arms when jumping and to get as low as possible when landing. Have her jump from the goal line to the top of the 18-yard box and back.

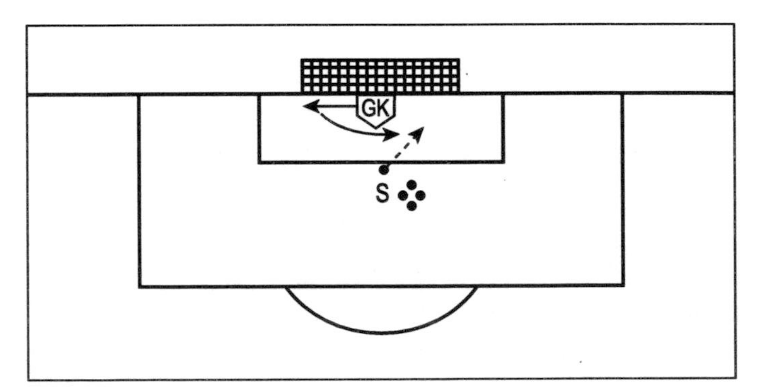

Figure 32-3

NEAR POST

Equipment Needed: 12 balls and 10 cones

Key Coaching Points: The keeper should land on her side and be sure her top hand is on top of the ball and her bottom hand is behind the ball. Stress the importance of letting the ball hit the ground first to cushion her fall and of using the ground as her third hand. Her bottom arm should come out and away from her body. After the ball, her shoulder—not her elbow—should hit the ground. She should keep her neck steady and straight. She should dive toward the ball at a forward angle and keep her bottom leg slightly bent once on the ground to maintain her balance on her side. The goalkeeper's top hand will have the best reach when power-diving. Encourage the keeper to always use two hands when possible. If she cannot save the shot with two hands, insist that she use a flat palm to redirect the ball out of bounds. The number-one rule of diving: only dive when necessary. Power-diving is also referred to as "high diving" or "extension diving."

Warm-Up Activities

□ Star

The goalkeeper begins in the center of the star, which is four yards in each direction from the center spot. She listens for a command from the server to move "Up," "Back," "Right," or "Left." The goalkeeper always begins and ends in the center of the star (see Figure 33-1). Have the keeper perform three intervals of 30 seconds. Stretch as needed between sets.

- For the first set, the server only gives one command at a time for the goalkeeper to respond to.
- For the second set, the server gives two commands at a time.
- For the third set, the server gives three commands at a time.

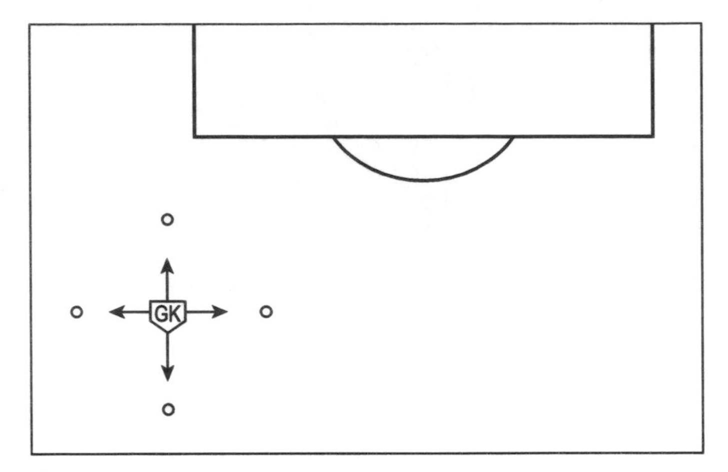

Figure 33-1

□ V-Sits

The goalkeeper sits on the ground with her legs out in front of her. The server gives an underhand toss to one side. The goalkeeper dives forward, trying to save the ball up toward her feet, creating a "V" when she saves the ball (see Figures 13-2 and 13-3 in Session #13). Perform two sets of 10. *Coaching Notes: V-sits help goalkeepers warm up in two ways. First, they warm up her hands, shoulders, and neck, thus preparing her upper body for the task of diving. Second, they prepare her mentally to always attack the ball and dive toward the ball at a forward angle.*

□ Over the Shoulder

The goalkeeper stands on the goal line in the middle of the goal. The server stands about three yards from the goalkeeper. With an underhand toss, the server distributes the ball over the goalkeeper's shoulder, just above her head. Using the opposite hand, the goalkeeper receives the ball, controls it, and then tosses it back, always using just the one hand (see Figures 33-2 and 33-3). Perform one set of 12 repetitions. *Coaching Notes: Make sure that the goalkeeper meets the ball while it is still in front of her. She should keep her arm straight and receive the ball at the highest point.*

□ Ball Gymnastics

Each goalkeeper has a ball. With legs spread slightly more than shoulder-width apart, she tries to catch the ball between her legs with one hand behind her legs and one hand in front of her legs (see Figure 27-4 in Session #27). Have the keeper perform one set of 20 repetitions for each exercise.

Figure 33-2

Figure 33-3

- For the first set, have her bounce the ball between her legs, and then quickly switch her hands to catch the ball between bounces.
- For the second set, challenge her not to let the ball hit the ground as she quickly switches her hands from front to back to catch the ball.

Near Post

Place a cone three yards in from the near post and three to six yards out from the goal line. The goalkeeper approaches the cone, and as soon as she is in front of the cone, the server directs the ball shoulder height between the near post and the cone (see Figure 33-4). Have the keeper perform two sets of six repetitions from each side of the goal. *Coaching Note: Depending on the level and age of your goalkeeper, adjust the distance of the cone away from the goal line (the closer the cone is to the goal, the easier the exercise).*

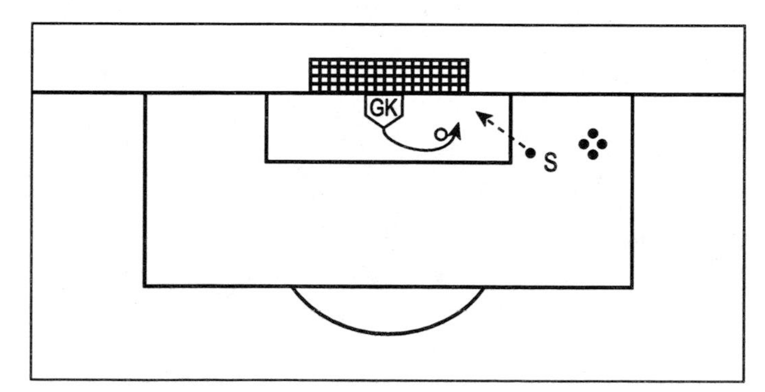

Figure 33-4

Near Post 1-2-3

Place a cone three yards in from the near post and three to six yards out from the goal line. The goalkeeper begins in the center of the goal on the goal line. To begin the exercise, the goalkeeper quickly shuffles to the near post, then shuffles to the cone. Once at the cone, she sets and the server directs the ball shoulder height between the near post and the cone (see Figure 33-5). Have the keeper perform two sets of six repetitions from each side of the goal.

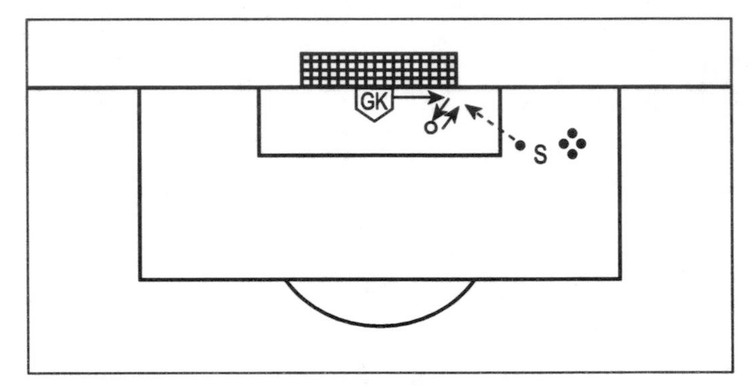

Figure 33-5

Strength/Fitness

Front Squat: Holding a ball in both hands with arms straight and away from her body, the goalkeeper performs a deep knee bend. Make sure her legs are shoulder width and she keeps her weight on her heels (see Figure 33-6). Have the keeper perform two sets of 15 repetitions.

Figure 33-6

Forward Lunge: In a standing position, the goalkeeper lunges forward onto her right leg and then pushes, only using her right leg, back to the standing position (see Figures 33-7 and 33-8). Have the keeper perform two sets of 12 repetitions.

Figure 33-7

Figure 33-8

FAR-POST SAVE

Equipment Needed: Eight cones and 12 balls

Key Coaching Points: The keeper should land on her side and be sure her top hand is on top of the ball and her bottom hand is behind the ball. Stress the importance of letting the ball hit the ground first to cushion her fall and to use the ground as her third hand. Her bottom arm should come out and away from her body. After the ball, her shoulder—not her elbow—should hit the ground. She should keep her neck steady and straight. She should dive toward the ball at a forward angle and keep her bottom leg slightly bent once on the ground to maintain her balance on her side. The goalkeeper's top hand will have the best reach when power-diving. Encourage the keeper to always use two hands when possible. If she cannot save the shot with two hands, insist that she use a flat palm to redirect the ball out of bounds. The number-one rule of diving: only dive when necessary. Power-diving is also referred to as "high diving" or "extension diving."

Warm-Up Activities

- Footwork

Place eight cones or balls two to three feet apart. Perform three sets of each exercise. Rest and stretch as needed between exercises.

In and Out: The starting positions to the side of the cones. With a slight bend in the knees, while balancing on the balls of her feet, the goalkeeper should weave in and out of the cones, keeping her hips square, head up, eyes forward, and hands ready (see Figure 5-1 in Session #5).

Power Step: The starting position is directly facing the line of cones, one step to the side. The leg nearest the cone power-steps forward on a slight angle through the cones. The trail leg should follow—but never touch—the other leg. After each power step through the cones, the goalkeeper should freeze for a second in the set position, meaning she is ready to react to a shot. Throughout the exercise, she should stay on the balls of her feet for balance, with her head up, eyes forward, knees slightly bent, and hands ready (see Figure 20-1 in Session #20).

Extended In and Out: Move every other cone one yard up so the cones make a zigzag pattern. The technique is the same as described in the In and Out exercise, except her first step should be big. The leg closest to the cone should be used to take the first step. Her first step should beat the cone. Be sure the goalkeeper keeps her balance when backpedaling by staying low and keeping her weight on the balls of her feet (see Figure 7-2 in Session #7).

□ Ball Gymnastics

Top Hand: The goalkeeper starts at cone 1 on her knees. The server tosses an underhand serve above her shoulder and about a half an arm's length away. The goalkeeper pins the ball to the ground with the hand furthest from the ball and should only use this hand (see Figures 32-1 and 32-2 in Session #32). Have the keeper perform one set of 12 to each side.

Two-Ball Toss: The goalkeepers stand facing each other one yard apart. They both take one large step to the right. To begin the exercise, both keepers toss the ball gently right in front of them, then each quickly steps to the side to catch the other keeper's ball. They continue this exercise non-stop for 20 seconds, rest and stretch for 40 seconds, and then do a second set for 20 seconds (see Figure 34-1 and 34-2).

Post-to-Post

Perform one set of six from each post. Remember to move the cone when switching sides of the goal.

Figure 34-1

Figure 34-2

- The goalkeeper begins with her shoulder on the right post, facing the sideline. About two thirds of the way in from the goalpost, place a cone on the goal line in order to shorten the goal. On the server's command, the keeper quickly turns and starts to shuffle across the goalmouth. Once the keeper is a step or so in toward the center of the goal, the server tosses the ball underhand and shoulder height, just inside the cone. The goalkeeper performs a power dive, and after making the save, she tosses the ball back to the server and quickly goes back to the right post (see Figure 34-3).
- Use the same set up as in the previous exercise, except the goalkeeper begins by lying on her stomach so her head is facing the sideline and her hips are level with the goalpost.

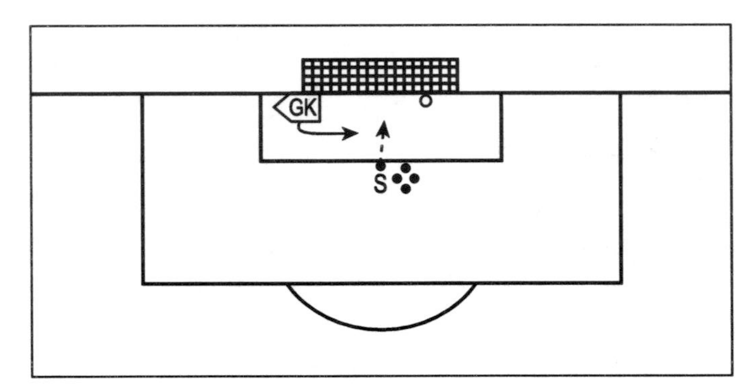

Figure 34-3

Pony

The non-working goalkeeper (the "pony") crouches down on all fours, making sure she protects her head with her hands, about three yards from the goal line in the center of the goal. The goalkeeper begins a step away and a step behind the pony. The server, who is about two yards away, tosses the ball underhand on the other side of the pony about a half a body's length and shoulder height. The goalkeeper takes a power step and power-dives over the pony to catch the ball (see Figures 34-4 through 34-7). Have the keeper perform one set of six on each side.

Strength/Fitness

Crunches: The goalkeeper lies on her back with knees bent and soles of feet flat on the ground. With her hands crossed on her chest, she brings her shoulders off the ground and points her nose to the sky. Have the keeper perform four sets of 25 repetitions.

Reverse Lunges: In a standing position the goalkeeper lunges backward with her right leg, and then only using her left leg returns to a standing position (see Figures 34-8 and 34-9). Have the keeper perform two sets of eight repetitions on each leg.

Figure 34-4

Figure 34-5

Figure 34-6

Figure 34-7

Figure 34-8

Figure 34-9

THE SECOND SAVE

Equipment Needed: Eight balls

Key Coaching Points: The keeper should land on her side and be sure her top hand is on top of the ball and her bottom hand is behind the ball. Stress the importance of letting the ball hit the ground first to cushion her fall and of using the ground as her third hand. Her bottom arm should come out and away from her body. After the ball, her shoulder—not her elbow—should hit the ground. She should keep her neck steady and straight. She should dive toward the ball at a forward angle, and keep her bottom leg slightly bent once on the ground to maintain her balance on her side. The goalkeeper's top hand will have the best reach when power-diving. Encourage the keeper to always use two hands when possible. If she cannot save the shot with two hands, insist that she use a flat palm to redirect the ball out of bounds. The number-one rule of diving: only dive when necessary. Power-diving is also referred to as "high diving" or "extension diving."

Warm-Up Activities

Stretch as needed between sets.

- Starting on the sideline, the goalkeepers jog across the width of the field and back twice.
- Starting on the sideline, the goalkeepers skip halfway across the field and shuffle to their right side the rest of the way. On the way back, they again skip halfway across the field and finish by shuffling to their left side. Have the keeper perform two sets there and back.
- Starting on the sideline, the goalkeepers stride the width of the field and back twice.

□ V-Sits

The goalkeeper sits on the ground with her legs out in front of her. The server gives an underhand toss to one side. The goalkeeper dives forward, trying to save the ball up toward her feet (see Figures 13-2 and 13-3 in Session #13). Have the keeper perform one set of 12. *Coaching Notes: V-sits help goalkeepers warm up in two ways. First, they warm up her hands, shoulders, and neck, thus preparing her upper body for the task of diving. Second, they prepare her mentally to always attack the ball and dive toward the ball at a forward angle.*

□ Over the Shoulder

The goalkeeper stands in the middle of the goal on the goal line. The server stands about three yards from the goalkeeper. With an underhand toss, the server distributes the ball over the goalkeeper's shoulder, just above her head. Using the opposite hand, the goalkeeper receives the ball, controls it, and tosses it back, always using just the one hand (see Figures 33-2 and 33-3 in Session #33). Have the keeper perform one set of 12.

□ Ball Gymnastics

- The goalkeeper stands with feet more than shoulder-width apart and weaves a ball on the ground in and out of her legs in a figure-eight pattern. Have the keeper perform one set at 20-second intervals in each direction.
- The goalkeeper stands with feet shoulder-width apart. Bent over with both hands on the ball, she tosses the ball between her legs, and then quickly moves her arms to the back of her legs to catch the ball before it hit the ground. Have the keeper perform two sets of 12 repetitions.

Same Side

The goalkeeper begins in the center of the goal, one yard off her goal line. The server stands just outside of the six-yard box, with a supply of balls. To begin the exercise, the server delivers a ball to the goalkeeper's right side at shoulder height, approximately a yard away from her body. As soon as the goalkeeper makes the save and is in the process of gaining her feet, the server delivers the second shot to the same side. After the second save is completed, the exercise continues to her left side. Continue to alternate sides (see Figure 35-1). Have the keeper perform two sets of eight repetitions (every serve equals one repetition).

Right-Left

Use the same set up as in the previous exercise, except after the goalkeeper makes the first save to the right side, the second serve is then quickly delivered to her left side. Make the first serve fairly easy and the second serve really challenge your goalkeeper. After every two serves, the goalkeeper goes back to the original starting point. Alternate the side of the easy serve and challenging serve. Have the keeper perform two sets of eight repetitions (every serve equals one repetition).

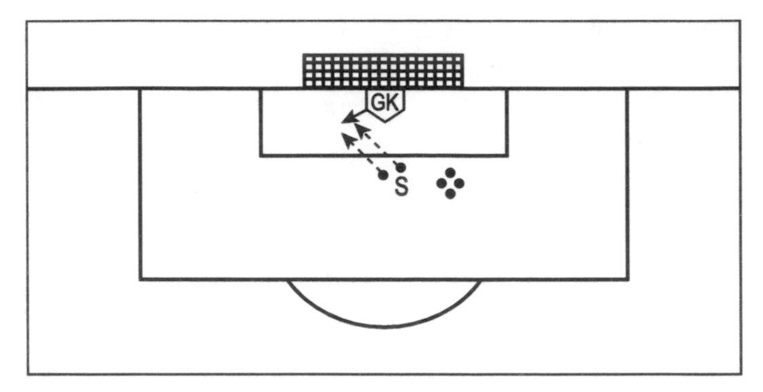

Figure 35-1

Strength/Fitness

Biceps/Triceps: The goalkeepers stand facing each other, with their hands touching (as shown in Figure 35-2). While one goalkeeper tries to push up, the other goalkeeper tries to push down. Have the keepers perform four 20-second intervals.

Back-to-Back Squats: The goalkeepers stand back to back. Together they squat low enough until their upper legs are parallel with the ground (see Figure 35-3) and then push back up together to the starting position. Have the keepers perform two sets of eight repetitions.

Figure 35-2

Figure 35-3

COMBINATION

Equipment Needed: 10 balls

Key Coaching Points: The keeper should land on her side and be sure her top hand is on top of the ball and her bottom hand is behind the ball. Stress the importance of letting the ball hit the ground first to cushion her fall and of using the ground as her third hand. Her bottom arm should come out and away from her body. After the ball, her shoulder—not her elbow—should hit the ground. She should keep her neck steady and straight. She should dive toward the ball at a forward angle and keep her bottom leg slightly bent once on the ground to maintain her balance on her side. The goalkeeper's top hand will have the best reach when power-diving. Always use two hands when possible. If she cannot save the shot with two hands, insist that she use a flat palm to redirect the ball out of bounds. The number-one rule of diving: only dive when necessary. Power-diving is also referred to as "high diving" or "extension diving."

Warm-Up Activities

Perform two 20-second intervals for each exercise. Stretch and rest as needed.

- One goalkeeper lies on their back with her legs apart, about six inches off the ground. The other goalkeeper stands between her legs. The goalkeeper on the ground closes her legs, which will cause the standing goalkeeper to jump and spread her legs. The goalkeeper on the ground sets the rhythm for the standing goalkeeper (see Figure 23-1 in Session #23).
- Same situation as in the previous exercise, except the goalkeeper on the ground keeps her legs apart the whole time, while the standing goalkeeper quickly side steps (with high knees) in and out of her legs (see Figure 23-2 in Session #23).
- Same situation as in the previous exercise, except the standing goalkeeper does a two-leg hop in and out of the other goalkeeper's legs as quickly as possible (see Figure 23-3 in Session #23).
- Same situation as in the previous exercise, except the standing goalkeeper jumps in and out on one leg.

- Ball Gymnastics

Perform two sets of 12 of each exercise.

- Each goalkeeper has a ball. They toss the ball straight up above their head and then catch the ball behind their backs. *Coaching Notes: Challenge them to throw the ball higher and higher. The trick to catching the ball behind your back is not to bend over.*
- Each goalkeeper has a ball. They hold the ball above and behind their head. They drop the ball, and then quickly bend down to catch the ball by reaching between their legs.

Low-High

The goalkeeper stands in the center of the goal about a yard off the goal line. The non-working goalkeeper stands 10 yards from the working goalkeeper, with a supply of balls. The server stands at the top of the six-yard box off to the right side, with a supply of balls. The non-working goalkeeper drives a hard shot right at the goalkeeper's legs. Soon after the goalkeeper saves the first shot, the server tosses a ball shoulder height a yard inside the near post (see Figure 36-1). Have the players perform a set of 10 repetitions to the right side, and then 10 to the left side. Every serve equals one repetition. Alternate the goalkeepers between each set.

Super Set

The goalkeeper begins in the middle of her goal about one yard off the goal line. The non-working goalkeeper is to her left at the top of the six-yard box and the server is to her right also at the top of the six-yard box, both with a supply of balls. The goalkeeper begins by shuffling over to face the non-working goalkeeper who will volley or toss a ball at head height at the goalkeeper. As soon as the goalkeeper makes the save, she quickly tosses the ball back to the non-working goalkeeper and shuffles across the

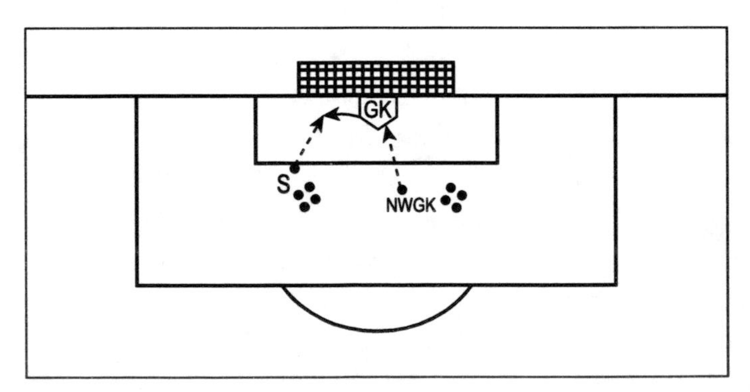

Figure 36-1

goalmouth. Once she reaches the center of the goal, again the server tosses a ball shoulder height just inside the near post (see Figure 36-2). Have the keepers perform two sets of eight repetitions. Every serve equals one repetition.

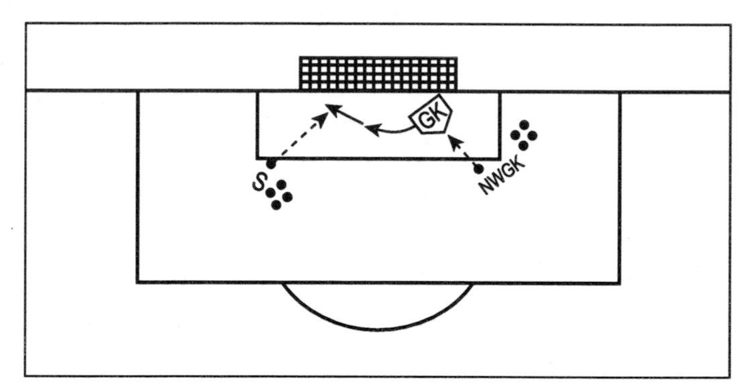

Figure 36-2

Strength/Fitness

Perform one set of 12 repetitions for each exercise.

- The goalkeeper is in a push-up position with arms fully extended. The non-working goalkeeper tosses her a ball at head height. The goalkeeper must catch the ball with one hand and toss it back (see Figure 36-3).
- The goalkeeper stands up on her arms and legs in a crab position. The non-working goalkeeper tosses her a ball just above her shoulders. The goalkeeper must catch the ball with one hand and toss it back (see Figure 36-4).

Figure 36-3

Figure 36-4

9

Tipping

TRAINING FOOTWORK

Equipment Needed: Five cones and 10 balls

Key Coaching Points: The first step for the goalkeeper when making this save should be backwards and in the line with the flight of the ball. She should try to keep her shoulders as square to the field as possible. Her hips should turn to be side on to the ball and feet staggered. It is important to stay on her feet as long as possible and tip the ball with the opposite hand. For example, if the ball is over her left side, she should tip the ball with her right hand

Warm-Up Activities

- Footwork

Quick Six: The goalkeeper begins at the right corner where the six-yard box meets the goal line. Facing the field, she shuffles across the goal line to the end of the six-yard box. She then sprints to the top of the six-yard box and quickly begins to shuffle across the top of the six facing the field. She finishes the repetition by backpedaling to the starting position (see Figure 37-1). Have the keeper perform three sets of three repetitions. Stretch as needed between sets

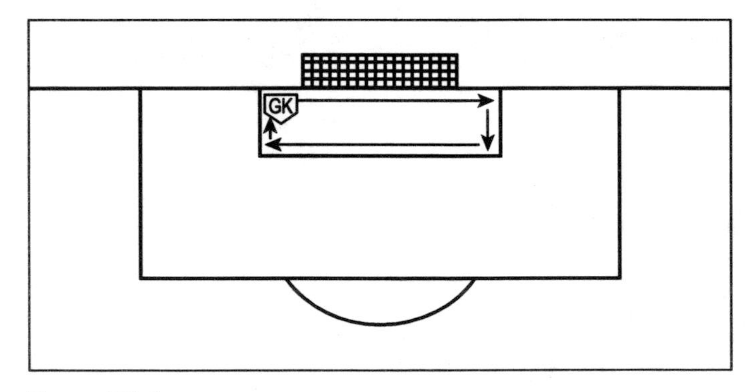

Figure 37-1

Hand to Crossbar: As shown in Figure 37-2, arrange five cones in an arc. The goalkeeper begins in the center of her goal, standing on the goal line. When ready, the goalkeeper approaches cone 1 the way she would come out of her goal to cut down the angle of an oncoming attacker. She touches the cone with her right hand, then quickly using a drop step, gets back to the starting position and tries to hit the back of her hand on the crossbar as if she were tipping a ball over. As soon as she is hits the crossbar and lands, she quickly approaches cone 2. She should use her right hand for cones 1, 2, and 3, and her left hand for cones 4 and 5. On the next set, have her begin with cone 5 first. Thus, she should use her left hand for cones 5, 4, and 3, and her right hand for cones 2 and 1. Have the keeper perform four sets. Alternate the goalkeepers between every two sets. *Coaching Note: When using the drop step, her feet should not cross or touch each other.*

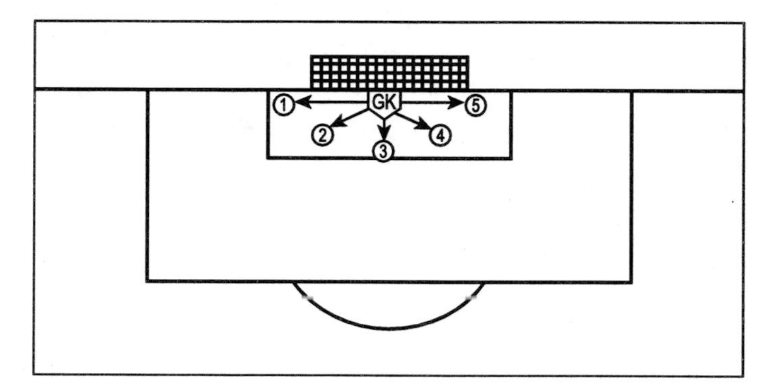

Figure 37-2

□ Over the Shoulder

The goalkeeper stands on the goal line in the middle of the goal. The server stands about three yards from the goalkeeper. With an underhand toss, the server distributes the ball over the goalkeeper's shoulder, just above her head. Using the opposite hand, the goalkeeper receives the ball, controls it, and then tosses it back, always using just the one hand (see Figures 33-2 and 33-3 in Session #33). Have the keeper perform two sets of 12. *Coaching Notes: Make sure that the goalkeeper meets the ball while it is still in front of her. She should keep her arm straight and receive the ball at the highest point.*

□ Ball Gymnastics

- The goalkeeper stands with a ball in her hands and her legs more than shoulder-width apart. In a figure-eight pattern, she weaves the ball at knee height between her legs. Perform two sets at 20-second intervals and rest for 20 to 40 seconds between sets.

- The goalkeeper stands with a ball in her hands and her legs shoulder-width apart. The goalkeeper bounces the ball between her legs, and then quickly moves her hands to catch the ball behind her. Perform two sets of 10.

Cone Tip

Place two balls at each cone. Using the same set up as the Hand to Crossbar exercise, the goalkeeper begins in the center of the goal standing on the goal line. When ready, she approaches cone 1. She tips the cone over with her right hand, and then quickly begins to drop. At that moment, the server tosses a ball above her head and over her left shoulder. The goalkeeper drops in a manner so the ball is always in front of her. With her right arm outstretched and palm facing the ball, the goalkeeper tips the ball over the crossbar (see Figures 37-3 through 37-6). Toss one ball per cone until she reaches the fifth cone. After the first save at the fifth cone, have her repeat the fifth cone and then proceed to finish the set. Have her use her right hand to tip the ball for cones 1, 2, and 3 and her left hand for cones 4 and 5. On the way back for the last five serves, have her use her left hand on cones 5, 4, and 3 and her right hand on cones 2 and 1. Perform four sets of 10.

Tipping Ladder

Place two balls in the center of the goalmouth four yards away, six yards away, and eight yards away (see Figure 37-7). The goalkeeper begins in the center of her goal on the goal line. When ready, the goalkeeper approaches the server who has a ball in her hands. The goalkeeper touches the ball with the hand with which she will tip (make sure she alternates the hand so she will receive equal practice on both her right and left side). Soon after the goalkeeper touches the ball and begins to drop, the server tosses the ball above her head just underneath the crossbar. The goalkeeper, using the same technique as described above in the Cone Tip drill, tips the ball over the crossbar. After the server tosses both balls at the four-yard distance, she quickly moves to the balls at the six-yard distance, then the eight-yard distance. Perform three sets of six. *Coaching Notes: The further the serve, the more challenging for your goalkeeper to get in position to tip the ball correctly. Encourage her to stay on her feet as long as possible. However, because of the pace of the ball, she may have to fully give in to the save and jump and extend in a way that she will land on the ground and not on her feet.*

Strength/Fitness

Russian Hammies: The working goalkeeper is on her knees. The non-working goalkeeper is behind her with her hands on the goalkeeper's heals. As slow as possible, the goalkeeper tries to lower herself to the ground. At the last possible second, she catches herself with her hands (see Figure 37-8). Have the keeper perform one set of eight.

Figure 37-3

Figure 37-4

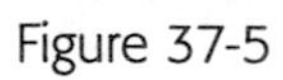

Figure 37-5

Figure 37-6

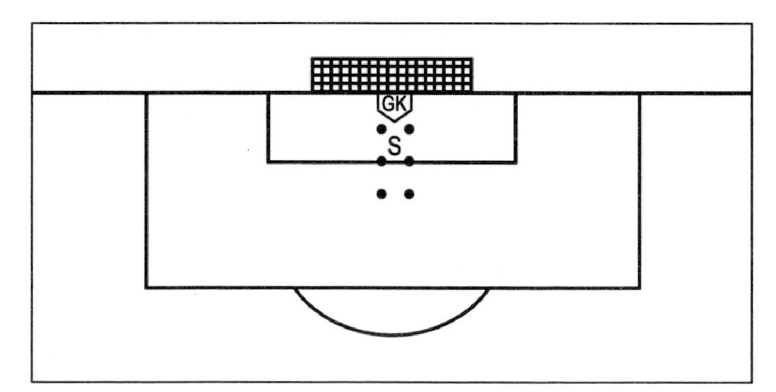

Figure 37-7

Elevator Push-Ups: In a push-up position, the goalkeepers listen for the following commands:

- "One"—the goalkeepers should be just inches from the ground.
- "Two"—the goalkeepers should be halfway up, thus their elbows should still have a slight bend.
- "Three"—the goalkeepers should be completely up with arms fully extended.

Their knees should never touch the ground and their backs should be straight. Have the keeper perform one set at a 30-second interval.

Figure 37-8

TRAINING THE TOP HAND

Equipment Needed: 12 balls

Key Coaching Points: The first step for the goalkeeper when making this save should be backwards and in the line with the flight of the ball. She should try to keep her shoulders as square to the field as possible. Her hips should turn to be side on to the ball and feet staggered. It is important to stay on her feet as long as possible and tip the ball with the opposite hand. For example, if the ball is over her left side, she should tip the ball with her right hand.

Warm-Up Activities

Place four balls randomly in the 18-yard box. The goalkeepers begin the warm-up by jogging around in the 18-yard box. On command, they perform the following exercises. Have them perform each activity twice. Rest and stretch as needed.

- Touch each ball once, and then continue jogging.
- Perform six toe taps on each ball, and then continue jogging.
- Lay flat on their backs next to each ball, and then continue jogging.

□ Over the Shoulder

The goalkeeper stands on the goal line in the middle of the goal. The server stands about three yards from the goalkeeper. With an underhand toss, the server distributes the ball over the goalkeeper's shoulder, just above her head. Using the opposite hand, the goalkeeper receives the ball, controls it, and then tosses it back, always using just the one hand (see Figures 33-2 and 33-3 in Session #33). Have the keeper perform two sets of 12 repetitions. *Coaching Notes: Make sure that the goalkeeper meets the ball while it is still in front of her. She should keep her arm straight and receive the ball at the highest point.*

- Ball Gymnastics

Stretch as needed between exercises.

- The goalkeeper stands with legs together and the ball in both hands held behind her knees. She tosses the ball up, quickly claps her hands in front of her legs, and then quickly reaches back to catch the ball. Have her perform two sets of 10.
- The goalkeeper stands with the ball held up by her face. She circles her head with the ball 10 times in one direction, and then 10 times the other way. She does the same around her waist, and ends with her closed legs. Have her perform two sets of 10 in both directions.

Toss and Tip

The server tosses a ball over the shoulder of the goalkeeper, who is on her knees (alternate the shoulder with each serve). The goalkeeper tips the ball as high and far back as possible. The non-working goalkeeper stands a couple of yards behind the goalkeeper and shags the balls (see Figures 38-1 through 38-3). Have the keepers perform two sets of 12.

Over the Crossbar

The goalkeeper stands in the middle of the goal on her goal line. The server is at the top of the six-yard box with a supply of balls. The goalkeeper comes out to the server who has the ball in her hands, and touches the ball with the hand she will use to tip the ball. After the goalkeeper touches the ball, she quickly drops to tip the ball, which the server tosses over her opposite shoulder (i.e., if the goalkeeper touches the ball with her right hand the ball is served over her left shoulder). The non-working goalkeeper stands behind the goal to shag the balls. Have the keeper perform three sets of six—one set in the center of the goal, one set on the right side of the goal, and one set on the left side of the goal (see Figure 38-4).

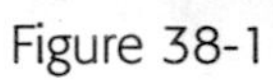

Figure 38-1

Figure 38-2

Figure 38-3

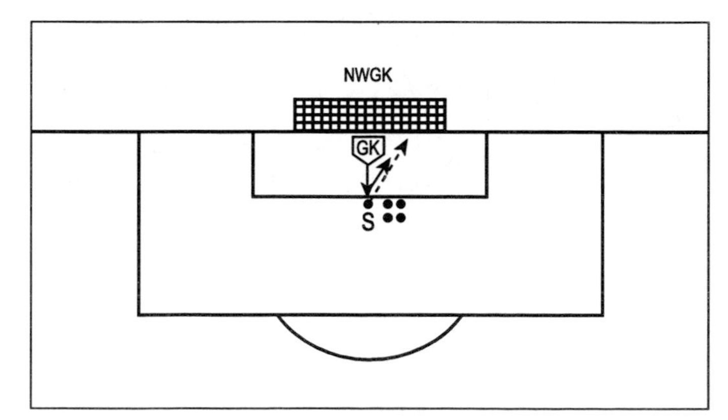

Figure 38-4

Strength/Fitness

Hip-Ups: The goalkeepers lay flat on their backs with their hands underneath their lower backs. With legs together, they push their feet up toward the sky until their hips come off the ground, and then bend their knees and push their legs out straight so they are parallel with the ground, always with legs together and off the ground (see Figures 38-5 and 38-6). Have the keepers perform one set of 30 repetitions.

Leap Frog: One goalkeeper begins is a frog position and the other goalkeeper uses her arms to leap over. Each goalkeeper should leap 12 times.

Figure 38-5

Figure 38-6

COMBINATION

Equipment Needed: Eight balls

Key Coaching Points: The first step for the goalkeeper when making this save should be backwards and in the line with the flight of the ball. She should try to keep her shoulders as square to the field as possible. Her hips should turn to be side on to the ball and feet staggered. It is important to stay on her feet as long as possible and tip the ball with the opposite hand. For example, if the ball is over her left side, she should tip the ball with her right hand.

Warm-Up Activities

- Footwork

Post-to-Post: The goalkeeper begins on the inside of the right goal post. On command, she quickly shuffles to the left post and then back to the right post eight times (count one repetition for every post). Have her perform three sets of eight repetitions. Stretch and rest as needed between sets.

- V-Sits

The goalkeeper sits on the ground with her legs out in front of her. The server gives her an underhand toss to one side. The goalkeeper dives toward the ball on an angle, trying to save the ball up toward her feet, creating a "V" when she saves the ball (see Figures 13-2 and 13-3 in Session #13). Have the keeper perform one set of 12. *Coaching Notes: V-sits help goalkeepers warm up in two ways. First, they warm up her hands, shoulders, and neck, thus preparing her upper body for the task of diving. Second, they prepare her mentally to always attack the ball and dive toward the ball at a forward angle.*

- Over the Shoulder

The goalkeeper stands on the goal line in the middle of the goal. The server stands about three yards from the goalkeeper. With an underhand toss, the server distributes the ball over the goalkeeper's shoulder, just above her head. Using the opposite hand, the goalkeeper receives the ball, controls it, and then tosses it back, always using just the one hand. Have her perform two sets of 12 repetitions. Stretch as needed. Coaching Notes: Make sure that the goalkeeper meets the ball while it is still in front of her. She should keep her arm straight and receive the ball at the highest point. (See Figures 33-2 and 33-3 in Session #33).

□ Ball Gymnastics

Have the keeper perform one set of six. Stretch and rest as needed between each set.

- Each goalkeeper has a ball. They toss the ball up in the air, quickly do a forward roll back to a standing position, and catch the ball before it hits the ground.
- Each goalkeeper has a ball. Sitting on the ground, they toss the ball up in the air and quickly stand up, without using their hands, to catch the ball before it hits the ground.

Near Post, Far Post

The goalkeeper begins the exercise in the center of the goal, one yard out from the goal line. The non-working goalkeeper is at the right corner of the six-yard box, and the server is standing in line with the near post at the top of the six-yard box, each with a supply of balls (see Figure 39-1). When ready, the goalkeeper shuffles over to the near post to receive a firm underhand toss from the non-working goalkeeper to the upper 90 (i.e., where the crossbar meets the goal post. Right after the tip save is made, the goalkeeper quickly shuffles back across the goalmouth to tip a firm underhand toss from the server. The toss from the server should be about two thirds of the way into the goal toward the far post. Perform two sets of eight on each side of the goal. Every serve equals one repetition.

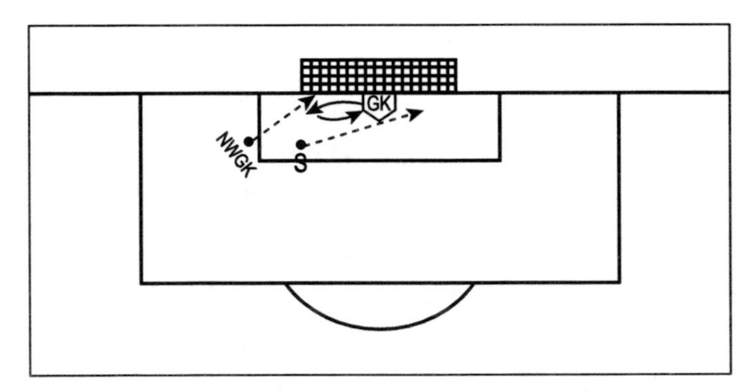

Figure 39-1

Combination

The goalkeeper begins the exercise in the center of the goal, about one yard off the goal line. The non-working goalkeeper is 12 yards away with a supply of balls. The server stands at the top of the six-yard box with a supply of balls (see Figure 39-2). The exercise begins with a hard-driven shot from the non-working goalkeeper right at the goalkeeper. As soon as the goalkeeper makes the save, she quickly prepares to tip a firm underhand toss from the server. Perform two sets of eight. Every serve equals one repetition. *Coaching Note: Service for the tip should be placed randomly to the right or left.*

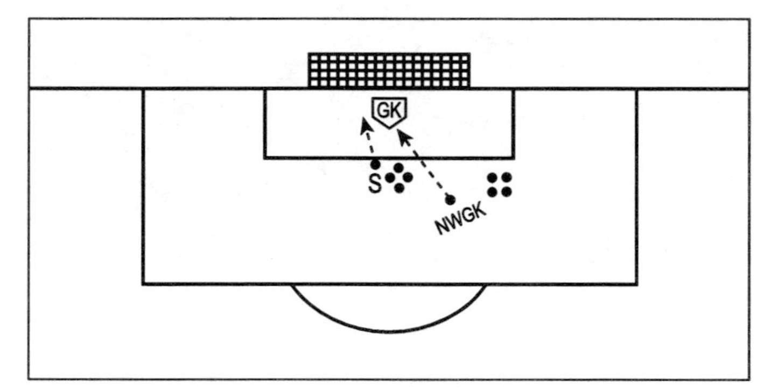

Figure 39-2

Strength/Fitness

Leg Lifts: Both goalkeepers begin the exercise flat on their backs with their hands tucked under their lower backs for support. They slowly raise their legs up and down. Once the exercise begins, their legs should not touch the ground (see Figures 39-3 and 39-4). Have them perform two sets of 15 repetitions.

Figure 39-3

Figure 39-4

Wheelbarrow Run: Have the goalkeepers race from the goal line to the top of the 18-yard box and back (see Figure 39-5). Have them perform two sets.

Figure 39-5

10

Distribution

OVERARM THROW AND BOWLING

Equipment Needed: 12 cones and eight balls

Key Coaching Points: When using the overhand throw, the goalkeeper should keep her arm straight and bring it up around her head. She should step in the direction that she is throwing, and bring her back leg forward as her arm comes around and she releases the ball. By doing this, she will maintain better balance and her throws will be more

Figure 40-1

Figure 40-2

Figure 40-3

accurate. Make sure she gets her whole body behind her throw and does not just throw with her arm (see Figures 40-1 through 40-3). When bowling, it is important to get low to the ground. To ensure a nice forward roll when releasing the ball, make sure her palm points to the sky (see Figures 40-4 through 40-6).

Warm-Up Activities

Perform each exercise for one minute. Stretch and rest as needed

Both goalkeepers jog around the 18-yard box with a ball in their hands. On command from the server, the keepers perform the following:

- Bowl the ball into space, and then quickly sprint to the ball to scoop it back up.
- Bowl the ball into space, and then quickly sprint to the other goalkeeper's ball and scoop it back up.

Figure 40-4

Figure 40-5

Figure 40-6

The goalkeepers stand 18 yards apart and using the overhand throw perform the following:

- Throw the ball at each other's feet.
- Throw the ball at chest height.

□ V-Sits

The goalkeeper sits on the ground with her legs out in front of her (see Figures 13-2 and 13-3 in Session #13). The server gives her an underhand toss to one side. The goalkeeper dives forward, trying to save the ball up toward her feet, creating a "V" when she saves the ball. Have her perform two sets of 12. *Coaching Notes: V-sits help goalkeepers warm up in two ways. First, they warm up her hands, shoulders, and neck, thus preparing her upper body for the task of diving. Second, they prepare her mentally to always attack the ball and dive toward the ball at a forward angle.*

□ Ball Gymnastics

Stretch and rest as needed.

- The goalkeeper stands with feet more than shoulder-width apart and weaves a ball on the ground in and out of her legs in a figure-eight pattern. Have her perform one set of 20 seconds in each direction.
- The goalkeeper stands with feet shoulder-width apart. Bent over with both hands on the ball, she tosses the ball between her legs, and then quickly moves her arms to the back of her legs to catch the ball before it hits the ground. Have her perform two sets of 12 repetitions.

Bowling and Throwing

Make six five-yard goals around the 18-yard box as illustrated in Figure 40-7. The goalkeeper begins in the goalmouth, the server is at the top of the 18-yard box with a supply of balls, and the non-working goalkeeper is at goal 1. The server gives a randomly placed shot on the goal. Once the goalkeeper makes the save, she bowls the ball through goal 1 to the non-working goalkeeper. As the goalkeeper prepares for the next shot, the non-working goalkeeper moves to goal 2, and so on. Bowl the ball through goals 1, 6, and 5. Throw the ball through goals 2, 3, and 4. Have the keepers perform three sets of six.

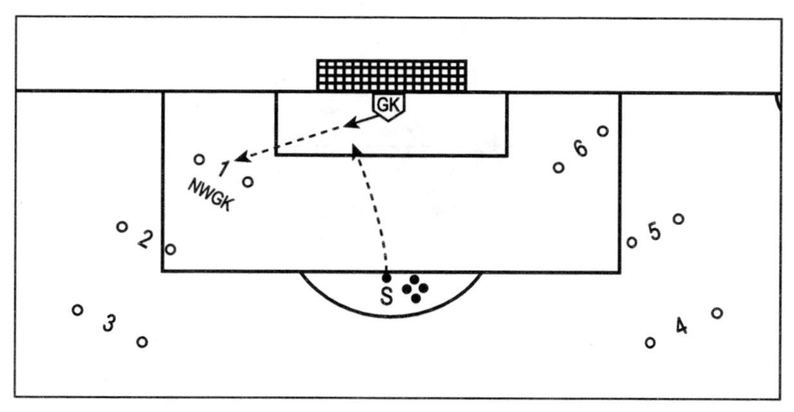

Figure 40-7

Goalkeeper War (Variation)

Place another full-size goal at the top of the 18-yard box. To decide who will have the ball first, have each goalkeeper bowl a ball from the goal line to the 18-yard line. The goalkeeper who is the closest to the line gets the ball first. To begin the game or to restart the game, the goalkeeper has to shoot within her six-yard box. A goalkeeper can only use the overhand throw or bowling techniques to score, and she must shoot where she makes the save. Have the keepers play two three-minute games.

Strength/Fitness

Roll-Out Push-Ups: The goalkeeper starts out with her legs shoulder-width apart, upper body bent down and her hands on a ball midway between her feet. She rolls forward on the ball until her body is in a push-up position. She performs a push-up, and then—without taking her hands off the ball or going down on her knees—she rolls back into the starting position (see Figure 2-6 in Session #2). Have her perform one set of 10.

Hungarian Sit-Ups: The goalkeepers sit close on the ground, facing opposite directions. Interlocking hands and keeping their legs straight and off the ground, they bring their legs up and around to the other side (see Figure 2-7 in Session #2). Have them perform two sets of 25.

GOAL KICKS

Equipment Needed: Eight cones and eight balls

Key Coaching Points: When taking goal kicks, five technical aspects are needed:

- Approach—should be six or more yards from the ball with a slight bend.
- Plant foot—should be about six inches from the ball and slightly behind the ball.
- Kicking leg—should use the full range of motion and have toe pointed and ankle locked. The foot of the kicking leg should strike the ball with the instep of the foot and kick the bottom, center of the ball.
- Follow-through—legs should stay separated during the swing and after the ball is kicked to ensure good balance. Goalkeeper should land on her kicking leg.
- Practice—Have your goalkeeper take eight to ten goal kicks before or after every practice (see Figures 41-1 through 41-3).

Warm-Up Activities

□ 5-Point Drill

Perform one set of each exercise at 20 seconds. Stretch and rest as needed between each exercise.

- Place five cones one yard apart (as shown in Figure 41-4). The goalkeeper stands with feet shoulder-width apart on points 1 and 2, jumps forward and brings legs together in the middle of point 3, jumps forward again and lands with feet shoulder-width apart on points 4 and 5. She then jumps backward and brings feet together on point 3, jumps backward again and lands with feet shoulder-width apart on points 1 and 2.
- Same idea as in the previous exercise, except when jumping forward or backward to point 3, only the right foot touches.
- Same idea as in the previous exercise, except when jumping forward or backward to point 3, only the left foot touches.

Figure 41-1

Figure 41-2

Figure 41-3

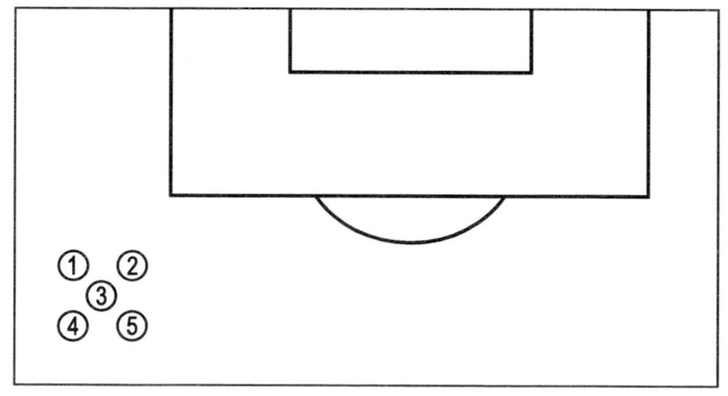

Figure 41-4

- Same idea as in the first exercise, except once on points 4 and 5 the goalkeeper does a half turn, landing on points 4 and 5 again before continuing. Once back to points 1 and 2, again a quick half turn before continuing to point 3.

□ Ball Gymnastics

Perform two sets of 12 of each exercise. Stretch and rest as needed.

- Each goalkeeper has a ball. They toss the ball straight up above their head and then catch the ball behind their backs. *Coaching Notes: Challenge them to throw the ball higher and higher. The trick to having them catch the ball behind their backs is not to bend over.*
- Each goalkeeper has a ball. They hold the ball above and behind their head. They drop the ball, and then quickly bend down to catch the ball by reaching between their legs.

Hit the Target

Make a 10-by-10-yard grid 30 yards from the goal line on both sides of the 18-yard box (see Figure 41-5). The goalkeeper tries to place her goal kick in the 10-yard box. If the goalkeeper puts the ball in the grid, she gets a point. If the non-working goalkeeper

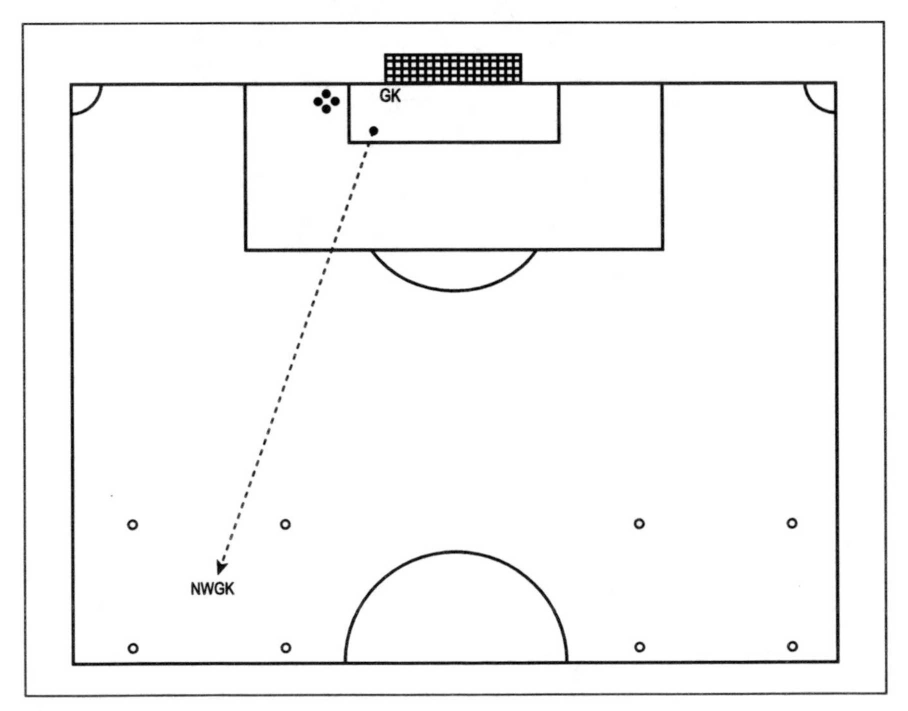

Figure 41-5

can trap the ball and keep it in the box, the non-working goalkeeper gets a point. Have them perform two sets of eight. The goalkeeper with the most points wins and the loser does 25 push-ups.

Best of Five

Each goalkeeper gets five goal kicks. The goalkeeper with the furthest kick wins. The loser does 25 push-ups. Have them play two games.

Strength/Fitness

Goalkeeper Lunges: The goalkeeper stands in a ready position. She lunges on a slight angle forward to her right side, and then brings her left foot back up to ready position (see Figures 13-9 and 13-10 in Session #13). Have her perform two sets of eight to each side. Rest as needed between each set.

Tuck Jumps: The goalkeeper stands with legs together. She does two hops and then quickly explodes up bring her knees to her chest (see Figure 13-11 in Session #13). Have her perform two sets of 10 with a two-minute rest between each set.

PUNTING AND DROP KICKS

Equipment Needed: Eight cones and eight balls

Key Coaching Points: When punting or drop kicking, four technical aspects are needed:

- Release of the ball—Whether using one hand or two, the ball should be released without spin.
- Kicking leg—Use full range of motion, with toe pointed and ankle locked. Foot should strike the bottom center of the ball. When drop kicking, contact with the ball should be made right after the ball makes contact with the ground, meaning just as the ball begins to come off the ground
- Follow-through—Legs should stay separated during the swing and after the ball is kicked to ensure good balance. Goalkeeper should land on her kicking leg.
- Practice—Have your goalkeeper take eight to ten punts and drop kicks before or after every practice (see Figures 42-1 through 42-8).

Figure 42-1

Figure 42-2

Figure 42-3

Figure 42-4

Figure 42-5

Figure 42-6

Figure 42-7

Figure 42-8

Warm-Up Activities

□ Plyometric Circuit

Have the goalkeepers perform two sets at 20-second intervals for each exercise. Rest and stretch as needed. *Coaching Notes: The goalkeepers should stay balanced by having a slight bend in their knees and their weight on the balls of their feet.*

- Each goalkeeper stands behind a ball. On "Go," they quickly tap the top of the ball with their right foot, knee coming up high, followed by their left foot. The ball should remain stationary.
- Each goalkeeper stands beside a ball. On "Go," they quickly jump laterally with legs together over the ball and back non-stop.
- Each goalkeeper stands behind a ball. On "Go," they quickly jump with legs together forward and back over the ball non-stop.

□ Ball Gymnastics

Stretch as needed between each exercise.

- The goalkeeper stands with a ball in her hands and her legs more than shoulder-width apart. In a figure-eight pattern, she weaves the ball at knee height between her legs. Have her perform two sets at 20-second intervals.
- The goalkeeper stands with a ball in her hands and her legs shoulder-width apart. The keeper bounces the ball between her legs, and then quickly moves her hands to catch the ball behind her. Have her perform two sets of 10.

Hit the Target II

Make a 15-by-15-yard grid at the halfway line on both sides of the 18-yard box (see Figure 42-9). The goalkeeper tries to place her punt or drop kick in the 15-yard box. If the goalkeeper hits the target, she gets a point. If the non-working goalkeeper can trap the ball and keep it in the box, the non-working goalkeeper gets a point. Have them perform two sets of eight, one with a punt and one set using the drop kick. The goalkeeper with the most points wins and the loser does 25 push-ups.

Best of Five II

Each goalkeeper gets five punts and five drop kicks. The goalkeeper with the furthest kick wins. The loser does 25 push-ups. Have them play two games, first game using the punt and the second game using the drop kick.

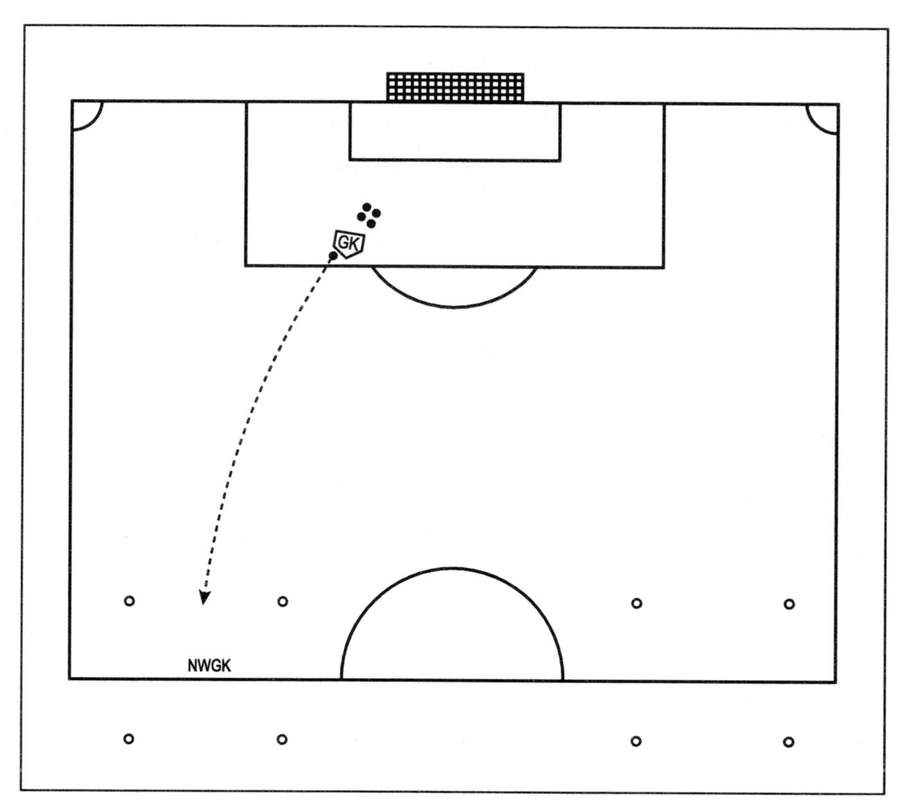

Figure 42-9

Strength/Fitness

AB Twist: The goalkeeper sits on the ground with her legs up, knees slightly bent. Holding a ball with both hands, she quickly twists from side to side bringing the ball down each time she twists to touch the ground (see Figure 14-3 in Session #14). Perform two sets of 30.

18-Yard Shuttle Run: Starting on the goal line, the goalkeepers sprint to the 18-yard line and back three times. Multiply the time it takes to perform one set by three and have them rest for that amount of time. Perform three sets.

DEALING WITH THE PASS BACK

Equipment Needed: Two cones and 12 balls

Key Coaching Points: Goalkeepers' foot skills have become a vital necessity of goalkeeping. The goalkeeper's role can no longer be viewed as a one-dimensional shot stopper. As with field players, solid foot skills have to be earned at practice. In addition to training your goalkeepers as goalkeepers, take time to train them as field players as well.

Warm-Up Activities

□ Feet Only

- Make a one-yard goal with two cones. The goalkeeper stands on one side of the goal and the server stands on the other side of the goal with a ball. The goalkeeper shuffles around one side of the goal and one-touch passes a ball back, using only feet, to the server. As soon as she passes the ball back, she shuffles to the other side of the goal for another one-touch pass. Repeat for 30 seconds. Have her perform two sets at 30-second intervals.
- The goalkeeper stands five yards from the server and the non-working goalkeeper stands five yards behind the server. The goalkeeper passes a ball to the server, who then passes back to the goalkeeper, who then passes to the non-working goalkeeper who is checking either one yard to the right or one yard to the left of the server. The non-working goalkeeper passes the ball back to the goalkeeper and the sequence continues. Have them perform two sets at 30-second intervals. Rotate the goalkeeper and non-working goalkeeper each set.

- Ball Gymnastics

Stretch and rest as needed between each exercise.

- The goalkeeper stands with legs together and the ball in both hands held behind her knees. She then tosses the ball up, quickly claps her hands in front of her legs, and then quickly reaches back to catch the ball. Have her perform two sets of 10.
- The goalkeeper stands with the ball held up by her face. She circles her head with the ball 10 times in one direction, and then 10 times the other way. She then does the same around her waist, and then her closed legs. Have her perform two sets of 10 in both directions.

Switch Fields

Set up a small goal outside of the 18-yard box. The goalkeeper begins the exercise in the goalmouth, the server is on the opposite side of the 18-yard box of the small goal, and the non-working goalkeeper is standing behind the small goal (see Figure 43-1). The goalkeeper receives a pass back from the server, which she must play through the small goal using no more than two touches on the ball. The server keeps a stopwatch from the first pass back to the last pass back. The goalkeeper with the lowest time wins (add one second for every pass that does not make it through the small goal). Have the loser do 25 push-ups. Have them perform two sets of 12 from each side of the field.

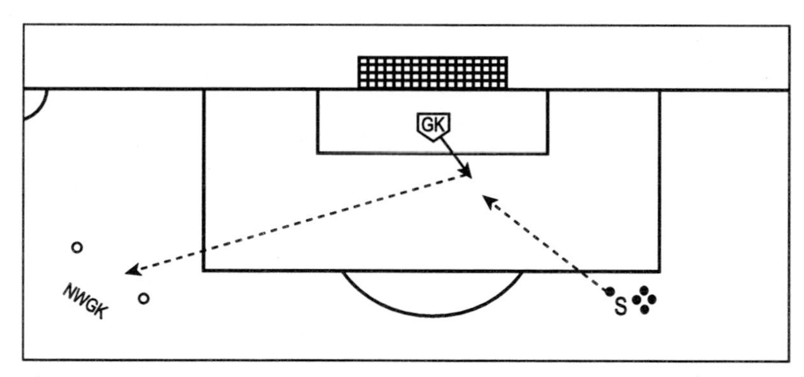

Figure 43-1

High, Far, Wide

The goalkeeper begins the exercise in the goalmouth, the server is at the top of the 18-yard box, and the non-working goalkeeper is standing behind the server. The server gives the goalkeeper a pass back. As soon as the server passes the ball, the non-working goalkeeper acts as an attacking player trying to win the ball and score. Using one to two touches, the goalkeeper clears the ball high, far, and wide. Have her perform two sets of 10.

Strength/Fitness

Front Squat: Holding a ball in both hands with arms straight and away from her body, the goalkeeper performs a deep knee bend. Make sure her legs are shoulder-width apart and she keeps her weight on her heels (see Figure 33-6 in Session #33). Perform two sets of 15.

Forward Lunge: In a standing position, the goalkeeper lunges forward onto her right leg and then pushes back to the standing position—using only her right leg. Have her perform two sets of 12.

FOOT SKILLS

Equipment Needed: 21 cones and six balls

Key Coaching Points: Goalkeepers' foot skills have become a vital necessity of goalkeeping. The goalkeeper's role can no longer be viewed as a one-dimensional shot stopper. As with field players, solid foot skills have to be earned at practice. In addition to training your goalkeepers as goalkeepers, take time to train them as field players as well.

Warm-Up Activities

□ Head to Toe

Goalkeepers stand one yard apart. Perform two sets of 12 for each exercise.

The non-working goalkeeper tosses a ball to the following areas:

- Toss the ball to the goalkeeper's right foot, who then one-touch passes it back to the non-working goalkeeper with her instep. Repeat to the left foot.
- Toss a ball so that the goalkeeper has to settle it with the top of her thigh, and then one-touch the ball back with the instep of her foot.
- Toss a ball so that the goalkeeper has to trap it with her chest, and then one-touch it back with the inside of the foot.
- Toss a ball so that the goalkeeper has to head it back.

□ Ball Gymnastics

Perform one set of eight. Rest and stretch as needed

- Each goalkeeper has a ball. They toss the ball up in the air, quickly do a forward roll back to a standing position, and settle the ball with their feet.
- Each goalkeeper has a ball. Sitting on the ground, they toss the ball up in the air, quickly stand up without using their hands, and settle the ball with their feet.

1v1

Place a cone in the center of the 18-yard box and have the goalkeepers play 1v1 using only their foot skills. You score a point by hitting the cone with the ball either by a pass or dribbling over the cone. The player with the most goals wins. The loser does 25 push-ups. Have them play three two-minute games.

Foot Skills Technical Circuit

Using a third of the field, set up the following circuits (as illustrated in Figure 44-1). The server should keep score for both goalkeepers. Each goalkeeper performs each circuit for a 20-second time interval. Go through each circuit twice.

- Circuit 1: The goalkeeper starts at cone 1, checks to cone 2, and to a one-touch pass given by the non-working goalkeeper. After the pass, the goalkeeper jogs back to cone 1 and repeats the process by checking to cone 3. To earn a point, the goalkeeper must pass the ball back in one touch and it must make it through the small goal.

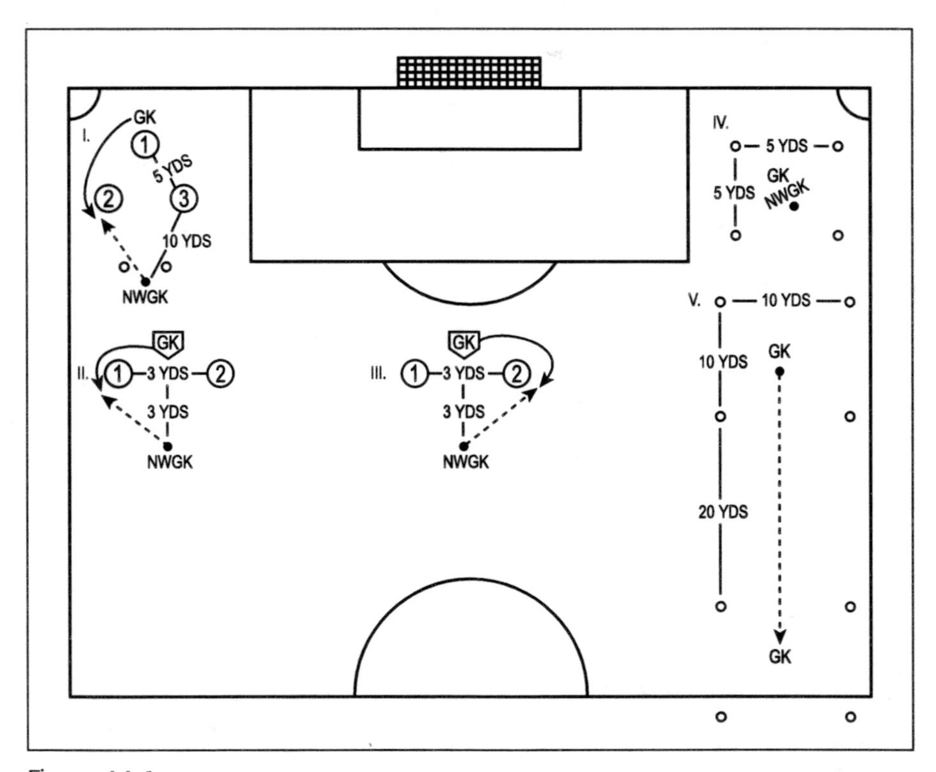

Figure 44-1

- Circuit 2: The goalkeeper shuffles around cone 1 to head the ball back to the non-working goalkeeper's hands. After the header, the goalkeeper quickly shuffles back around to cone 2 and repeats the process. To earn a point, the non-working goalkeeper must catch the header.
- Circuit 3: The goalkeeper shuffles around a cone to perform a one-touch pass. To earn a point, the pass must go right to the non-working goalkeeper's feet.
- Circuit 4: Both goalkeepers are in the five-by-five-yard grid. The object is to win the ball from the non-working goalkeeper and kick it out of the grid. Every time the ball is kicked out of the grid or the non-working goalkeeper dribbles out of the grid, the goalkeeper gets a point.
- Circuit 5: Each goalkeeper takes turns sending a long ball to the other grid. If the receiving goalkeeper can trap the ball and keep it in the grid, the goalkeeper who kicked the ball gets a point.

Strength/Fitness

Hand Slaps: With gloves off, the goalkeepers face each other in a push-up position. On "Go," they each try to slap the other's hand. Their backs should stay straight and they should not go down on their knees (see Figure 3-4 in Session #3). Perform two sets at 20-second intervals each. Give them at least 40 seconds rest between each set.

Goalkeeper Sit-Ups: The goalkeepers lay on their backs with feet touching. Using one ball, they take turns throwing the ball back and forth, doing a sit-up every time they catch the ball (see Figure 3-5 in Session #3). Have them perform two sets of 25 reps.

11

Free Kicks

PENALTY KICK

Equipment Needed: Five balls and eight cones

Key Coaching Points: In general you have three types of kickers.

- A power kicker, who is identified by their long approach and bend in their run (see Figure 45-1).
- A finesse kicker, who is identified by a shorter approach that is usually straight behind the ball (see Figure 45-2).
- A pre-determined kicker, who is someone who always kicks to the same place. Unless the coach or goalkeeper has seen a player several times the per-determined kicker is difficult to identify and will probably not come into use until maybe at the college level and usually at the professional level when scouting is more prevalent.

Warm-Up Activities

□ Footwork

Place eight cones or balls two feet to one yard a part. Have the keeper perform three sets of each exercise. Stretch and rest as needed.

Figure 45-1

Figure 45-2

In and Out: The starting position is to the side of the cones. With a slight bend in the knees, while balancing on the balls of the feet, the goalkeeper should weave in and out of the cones keeping her hips square, head up, eyes forward, and hands ready (see Figure 5-1 in Session #5).

Up and Over: The starting position is to the side of the cones. The leg nearest to the cone goes over first, and then the second leg follows. With her knees coming up high, the goalkeeper should go up and over each cone, keeping her hips square, head up, eyes forward, and hands ready. Her feet should not touch or cross each other (see Figure 5-2 in Session #5).

Power Step: The starting position is directly facing the line of cones, one step to the side. The leg nearest the cone power-steps forward on a slight angle through the cones. The trail leg should follow—but never touch—the other leg. After each power step through the cones, the goalkeeper should freeze for a second in the set position, meaning she is ready to react to a shot. Throughout the exercise, she should stay on the balls of her feet for balance, with her head up, eyes forward, knees slightly bent, and hands ready (see Figure 20-1 in Session #20).

Extended In and Out: Move every other cone one yard up so the cones make a zigzag pattern. The technique is the same as described in the In and Out exercise, except her first step should be big. The leg closest to the cone should be used to take the first step. Her first step should beat the cone. Be sure the goalkeeper keeps her balance when backpedaling (see Figure 7-2 in Session #7).

- Ball Gymnastics

Stretch and rest as needed between exercises.

Reverse Diving: One goalkeeper is standing with a ball in her hands. The other goalkeeper is lying on the ground on her side. The keeper with the ball tosses the ball up in the air so that the keeper on the ground can quickly get up and catch the ball before it hits the ground. As soon as the keeper with the ball tosses the ball in the air, she quickly dives on the ground, staying on her side as if low-diving to a ball. Make sure they alternate the side on which they dive down. They continue this exercise until each keeper has gone 10 times.

Hike: Each goalkeeper has a ball. Standing with her legs shoulder-width apart, she hikes the ball up between her legs so that the ball comes up and around her back and over her shoulder so she is able to catch the ball. Make sure she alternates the shoulder the ball goes over. Have her perform one set of 12 repetitions.

Confidence Builder

The goalkeeper stands on her goal line, the server is set to take the penalty kick and the non-working goalkeeper stands behind the goal in a position so she can see the server taking the kick. The server tells the goalkeeper where she will kick the ball. The goalkeeper should focus on making the save, and the non-working goalkeeper studies the body movement of the server. Have the keeper perform two sets of 10. *Coaching Notes: In addition to the type of kicker, a goalkeeper can use other clues to help read where the ball is going. In general, if the kicker leans over the ball, it will stay low, and if she is straight up or leaning back, the ball will be in the air. For example, a right-footed power kicker who follows through the ball by swinging her leg across her body will either kick the ball at the goalkeeper or to the goalkeeper's right side. The more a goalkeeper analyzes the approach and body movements, the more informed they will be when making their decision.*

Shoot Out

Each goalkeeper gets five penalty kicks on the other goalkeeper. The goalkeeper who gives up the fewest goals wins. If tied after five kicks each, continue with sudden-death penalty kicks. Have the loser do 25 push-ups. Play two rounds.

Strength/Fitness

AB Twist: The goalkeeper sits on the ground with her legs up and her knees slightly bent. Holding a ball with both hands, she quickly twists from side to side, bringing the ball down each time she twists to touch the ground (see Figure 14-3 in Session #14).

18-Yard Shuttle Run: Starting on the goal line, the goalkeepers sprint to the 18-yard line and back three times. Multiply the time it takes to perform one set by three and have them rest for that amount of time. Have them perform three sets.

SETTING UP WALLS

Equipment Needed: You will need four field players, eight cones, and eight balls

Key Coaching Points: Being able to quickly set up a wall to defend against a free kick takes a lot of focus and good direction from your goalkeeper. All players on the team should know what is expected from them in this situation. The moment the goalkeeper hears the whistle blow on a free kick, she should say the following in a specific and commanding tone. Yell out the number of players to be used in the wall (see Figure 46-1). If no wall is used, then specify where the line of defense should be. Time permitting, quickly go to the near post and line up the post player so that half of her body is beyond the near post (it is easier for the post person to face the goalkeeper and have the goalkeeper point the post player into position). If an indirect kick is in a dangerous position, direct the last player in the wall to act as a bullet. As soon as the ball is touched, the bullet player should sprint toward the ball. Direct the rest of the players to mark goal side and—most importantly—stay in the same line as the wall. Remember, offside applies on a free kick (see Figure 46-2).

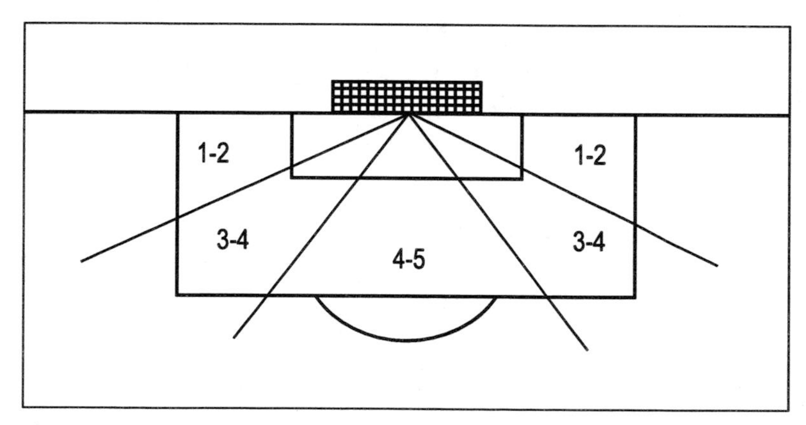

Figure 46-1

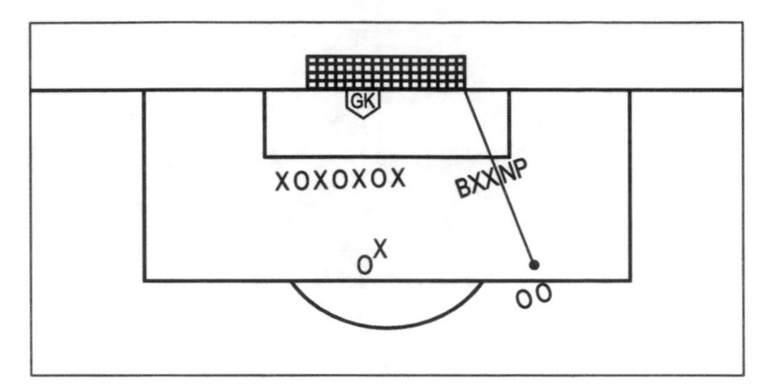

Figure 46-2

Warm-Up Activities

□ Footwork

Using the six-yard box, have the keeper perform the following exercises (see Figure 46-3). Perform each exercise three times. Rest and stretch as needed between exercises

- The goalkeeper starts at the right goalpost. On "Go," she quickly shuffles to the left goalpost, then sprints diagonally to cone 1, then shuffles to cone 2, then backpedals back on a diagonal to the right goalpost.
- Use the same progression as in the previous exercise, except have her start at the left goal post.

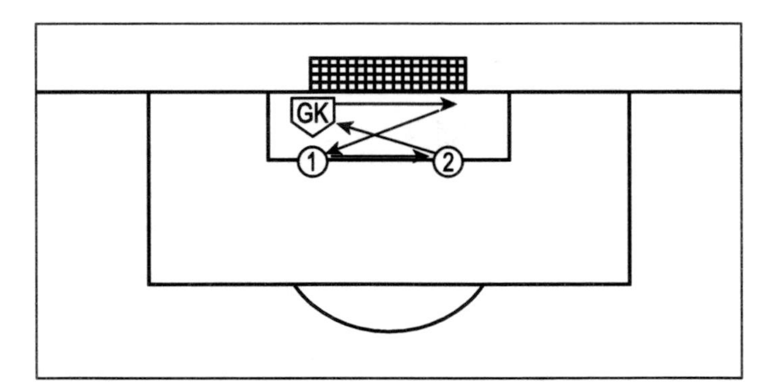

Figure 46-3

□ Diving Circuit

Perform one set of 12 for each exercise

V-Sits: The goalkeeper sits on the ground with her legs out in front of her (as shown in

Figures 13-2 and 13-3 in Session #13). The server gives her an underhand toss to one side. The goalkeeper dives at a forward angle, trying to save the ball up toward her feet, creating a "V" when she saves the ball. Coaching Notes: V-sits help goalkeepers warm up in two ways. First, they warm up her hands, shoulders, and neck, thus preparing her upper body for the task of diving. Second, they prepare her mentally to always attack the ball and dive toward the ball at a forward angle.

Kneeling: The goalkeeper kneels on the ground, and the server strikes a ball at face or chest level. Serves should steadily increase in velocity (see Figure 13-3 in Session #13). *Coaching Notes: This exercise is great for improving hand and arm strength. The kneeling position forces the keeper to use her hands and arms, instead of relying on the balance and strength of her legs.*

Standing: From a standing position, the goalkeeper performs a low dive using one step (see Figures 13-4 through 13-6 in Session #13).

- ☐ Ball Gymnastics

- The goalkeeper sits on the ground with her legs straight and spread wide. She rolls the ball around her feet slowly five times in one direction, and then five more times in the opposite direction.
- The goalkeeper sits on the ground with her legs straight and spread wide. She twists around and places the ball behind her back, then twists in the opposite direction to retrieve the ball. Have her do five twists with the ball in both directions.

Five-Second Drill

Scatter eight balls inside and outside the 18-yard box. Have the four field players and the non-working goalkeeper jog around the top of the 18-yard box (see Figure 46-4). The server points to a ball and indicates with her arm if it is a direct kick (arm held

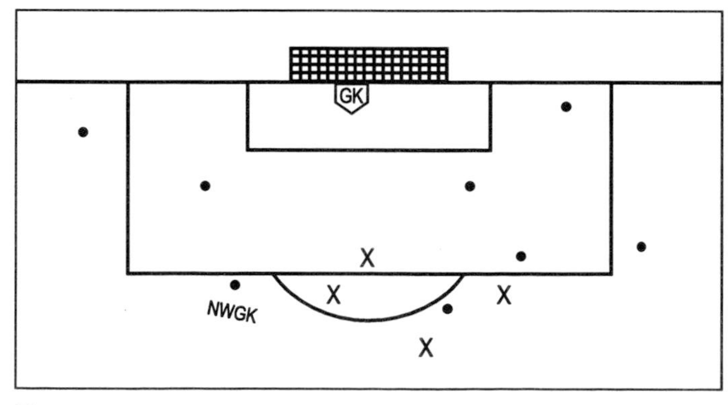

Figure 46-4

straight out at shoulder height) or an indirect kick (arm held straight up). The goalkeeper has five seconds to set up the wall. Once the server indicates a ball, she begins the five-second count out loud. No shot is taken. Perform two sets of eight.

Ready or Not

Use the same set up as in the previous exercise, except at the five-second mark the server takes the shot whether the goalkeeper is ready or not. Perform two sets of eight.

Strength/Fitness

Protect Your Baby: One keeper has a ball tucked in her arms. The other keeper may do anything except spit on, punch, tickle, or kick to get the ball. The keeper holding on to the ball must stand in the same spot. If the non-working goalkeeper gets the ball from the keeper, she gives it right back. The keeper who manages to hold on to her "baby" and loses possession the fewest times wins. Each keeper gets two turns to hold on to the ball for 30 seconds.

Human Hurdles: The goalkeepers lay on their stomachs side by side. Goalkeeper one dives over goalkeeper two. They continue this process until each keeper has gone 10 times. After a one-minute rest, they do a second set back to their original starting position (see Figures 6-3 and 6-4 in Session #6).

CORNER KICKS

Equipment Needed: 10 field players, two full-size goals, eight cones, and 10 balls.

Key Coaching Points: The moment your goalkeeper determines a corner kick is coming, she should communicate the following. Organize the "defensive shell" and the remaining players in a goal-side marking position. Once the ball is kicked, she should yell, "Keeper," if leaving the line to play the ball, or, "Away," if holding the line. Once the ball is safely away or saved, she should command that everyone, including the post players, push up out of the 18-yard box. The near-post player (NP) should stand up straight with her shoulder tight on the post, facing the ball. The short player (SP) should be 10 yards from the ball and one yard in from the goal line. By organizing the near-post player and short player this way, a two-player wall is created, which allows the goalkeeper (GK) to cheat forward a little. Although many opinions exist on how to place your post player, the following is the most effective way. Place the far-post player (FP) one step inside the goal, because it is easier to step forward, jump, and head the ball out than to bend backwards. The player at the top of the six-yard box (6P) should be your strongest player in the air with her head. Of course, covering your back door (BD) is always important. The goalkeeper should be halfway or two-thirds of the way back in the goal—again because it is easier to step forward, jump, and save the ball than to scramble backwards. The goalkeeper should be in an open position, facing the field. Doing so will give her the ability to see the whole field and to move quickly in any direction.

Warm-Up Activities

- Footwork

Place eight balls or cones in a row two to three feet apart. Perform three sets of each exercise. Stretch as needed between exercises.

High Knees: The starting position is facing the cones. At speed, the goalkeeper goes over each cone, bringing her knees up high, taking one quick step between each cone. Once at the end, she quickly backpedals to the starting point.

Two-Leg Jump: The starting position is facing the cones. With legs together, the goalkeeper tries to jump up and over each cone. She should focus on the height of her jump and not how quickly she jumps over the cones.

One-Leg Jump: The starting position is facing the cones. On one leg, the goalkeeper tries to jump as high as possible over each cone. Encourage her to use her arms and non-working leg to get as high as possible.

Pattern Jumping: The starting position is beside the first cone. With legs together, the goalkeeper jumps over the first cone then up to the second cone, over the second cone and up to the third cone, and so on.

□ Highest Point

Place three cones in a triangle approximately one yard apart. The goalkeeper begins at the top of the triangle, and the server stands around three yards from the bottom of the triangle with a supply of balls. The server tosses a high ball over cone 2. The goalkeeper tries to catch the ball above her head at the highest point. Continue this exercise by the goalkeeper backpedaling to cone one and the server then tosses a ball over cone 3. As the goalkeeper is backpedaling, the non-working goalkeeper shifts over to cone 3 (see Figure 47-1). Have the keeper perform two sets of eight. *Coaching Note: Make sure she brings the leg closest to the cone in the high-knee position to help her achieve maximum height in her jump.*

□ V-Sits

The goalkeeper sits on the ground with her legs out in front of her (as shown in Figures 13-2 and 13-3 in Session #13). The server gives her an underhand toss to one side. The goalkeeper dives at a forward angle toward the ball, trying to save the

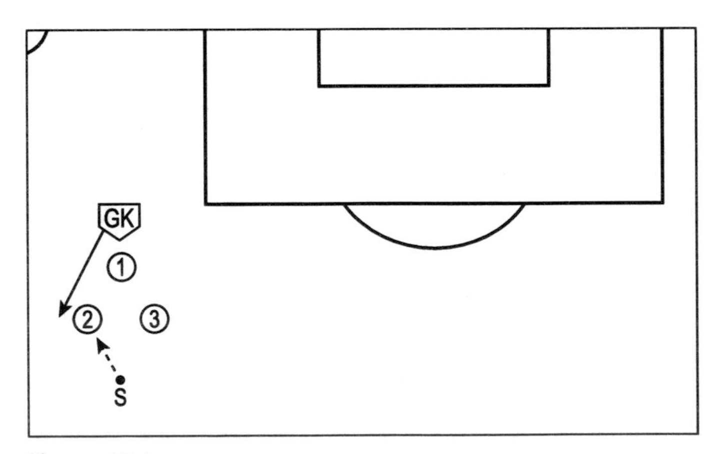

Figure 47-1

ball up toward her feet, creating a V when she saves the ball. Perform one set of 12. *Coaching Notes: V-sits help goalkeepers warm up in two ways. First, they warm up her hands, shoulders, and neck, thus preparing her upper body for the task of diving. Second, they prepare her mentally to always attack the ball and dive toward the ball at a forward angle.*

□ Ball Gymnastics

- The goalkeeper stands with feet more than shoulder-width apart and weaves a ball on the ground in and out of her legs in a figure-eight pattern. Have her perform one set at 20-second intervals in each direction.
- The goalkeeper stands with feet shoulder-width apart. Bent over with both hands on the ball, she tosses the ball between her legs, and then quickly moves her arms to the back of her legs to catch the ball before it hit the ground. Have her perform two sets of 12 repetitions.

Best of Ten

Split your 12 players (10 field players and two goalkeepers) into two teams of six. One team is on offense and the other on defense. Before each corner kick, all players are jogging around the 18-yard box. When the server shouts "Go," one player on the offensive team sprints off the field to take the corner kick, giving the goalkeeper time to organize her team in the "defensive shell" (see Figure 47-2). As soon as the kicker is ready, she can take the corner kick. Each team gets ten corner kicks, five from each side of the field. The defensive team that gives up the fewest goals wins. Play this game twice.

Corner-Kick Game

Extend the 18-yard box out to 30 yards and place a second full-size goal on the 30-yard line (see Figure 47-3). One player for each team stands at a corner-kick spot with

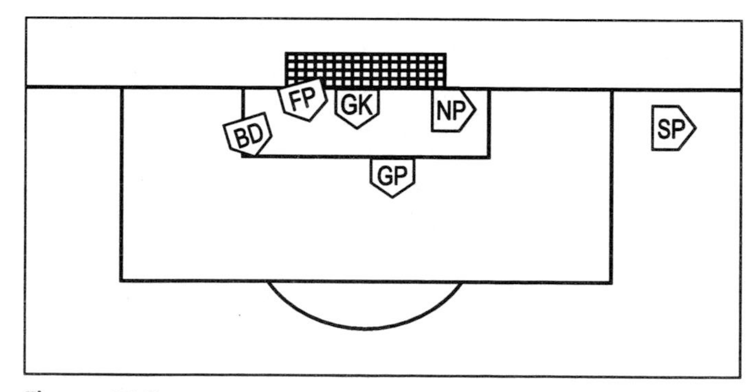

Figure 47-2

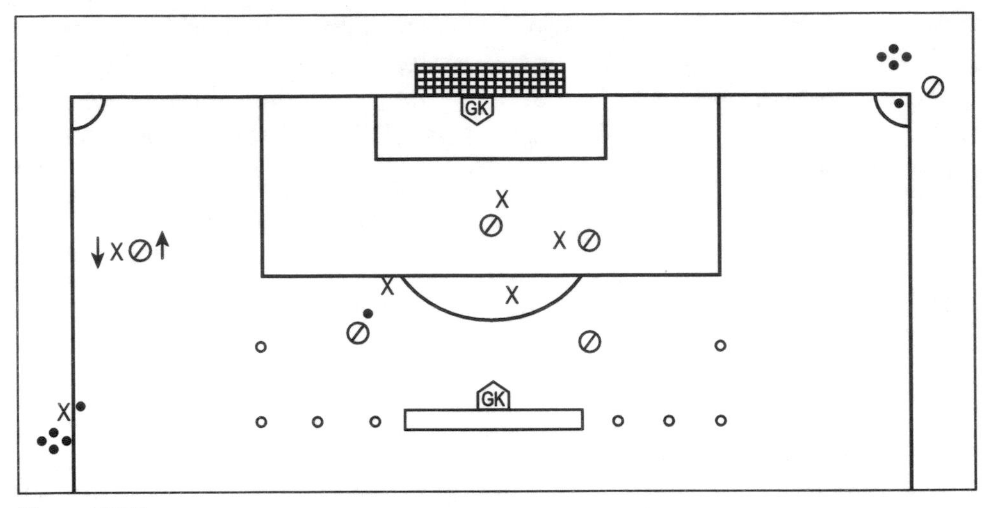

Figure 47-3

a supply of balls. The rest of the players play 4v4 plus goalkeepers. Every restart is with a corner kick. Thus, if a team wins a throw-in, scores a goal, or earns a corner kick or a goal kick, they are given a corner kick. Rotate the server every five minutes. Each time a server is rotated, have her switch the side of the field from which she is taking the corner kick. Play one 20-minute game.

Strength/Fitness

Russian Hammies: The working goalkeeper in on her knees. The non-working goalkeeper is behind her with her hands on the goalkeeper's heels. As slow as possible, the goalkeeper tries to lower herself to the ground. At the last possible second, she catches herself with her hands (see Figure 37-8 in Session #37). Have her perform one set of eight.

Elevator Push-Ups: In a push-up position, the goalkeepers listen for the following commands:

- "One"—the goalkeepers should be just inches from the ground.
- "Two"—the goalkeepers should be halfway up, thus their elbows should still have a slight bend.
- "Three"—the goalkeepers should be completely up with arms fully extended. Their knees should never touch the ground and their backs should be straight. Have them perform one set at a 30-second interval.

12

Pressure Training

BUILDING STRENGTH

"It takes the hammer of practice to drive the nail of success."

—Author unknown

Equipment Needed: 10 balls

Warm-Up Activities

Randomly scatter four balls in the 18-yard box. Both goalkeepers jog around in the 18-yard box and perform the following when the server yells, "Go." After each repetition, the goalkeepers should continue jogging until the server yells, "Go," again. Have them perform each exercise for 30 seconds. *Coaching Note: Give at least 20 seconds between exercises for recovery.*

- Sprint to each ball and touch with one hand.
- Perform a lateral jump over and back over each ball.
- Do a push-up next to each ball.
- Lay flat on her back next to each ball.
- Perform a low dive on each ball.

□ Ball Gymnastics

Stretch as needed between each exercise.

Reverse Diving: One goalkeeper is standing with a ball in her hands. The other goalkeeper is lying on the ground on her side. The keeper with the ball tosses the ball up in the air so that the keeper on the ground can quickly get up and catch the ball before it hits the ground. As soon as the keeper with the ball tosses the ball in the air, she quickly dives on the ground, staying on her side as if low-diving to a ball. Make sure they alternate the side on which they dive down. They continue this exercise until each keeper has gone 10 times.

Hike: Each goalkeeper has a ball. Standing with her legs shoulder-width apart, she hikes the ball up between her legs so that the ball comes up and around her back and over her shoulder so she is able to catch the ball. Make sure she alternates the shoulder over which the ball goes. Perform one set of 12 repetitions.

20-Second Drill

The goalkeeper is in the goalmouth two to three yards off the goal line. The server is around 12 yards away with a supply of balls. At 20-second intervals, the goalkeeper performs the goalkeeper exercises. While the goalkeeper is working, the non-working goalkeeper has active rest and performs the non-working goalkeeper exercises. Rotate the goalkeeper and non-working goalkeeper after each exercise. Have them perform three sets of each exercise.

Goalkeeper Exercises

- Exercise #1: Shot stopping with balls served at the feet
- Exercise #2: Shot stopping with balls served at waist height
- Exercise #3: Shot stopping with balls served at chest height

Non-Working Goalkeeper Exercises

- Exercise #1: Jogging
- Exercise #2: Crunches
- Exercise #3: Push-ups

Around the World

Arrange 10 balls around the 18-yard box (see Figure 48-1). The server should give the goalkeeper just enough time to get on her feet before each shot. Rotate the goalkeeper and non-working goalkeeper after each exercise. Have them perform one set of each exercise (one set equals the time it takes the server to take 10 shots on the goalkeeper). While the goalkeeper is working, the non-working goalkeeper has active rest and performs the non-working goalkeeper exercises.

Goalkeeper Exercises

- Shot stopping, starting each shot in a sitting position
- Shot stopping, starting each shot in a push-up position
- Shot stopping, starting each shot flat on their back

Non-Working Goalkeeper Exercises

- Sprint 10 yards and jog back.
- Backpedal 10 yards and jog back.
- Shuffle 10 yards and jog back.

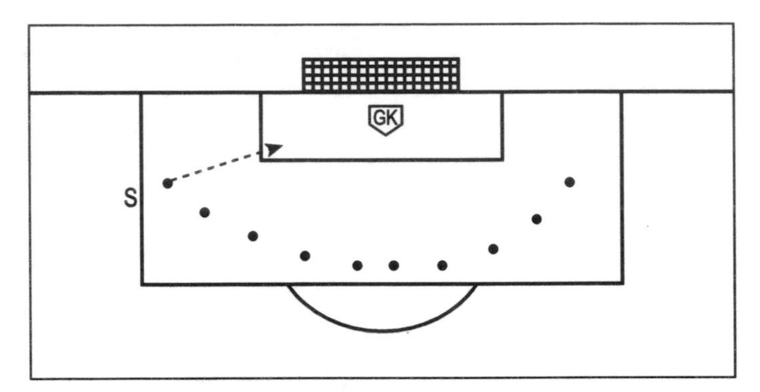

Figure 48-1

Strength/Fitness

Side to Side: The goalkeeper stands with legs apart slightly more than shoulder width and hands behind her head. She shifts all of her weight to her right leg until her knee is in line with her toe, and then slowly shifts all of her weight to her left leg (see Figures 24-2 and 24-3 in Session #24). Have her perform two sets at 30-second intervals.

Good Mornings: The goalkeeper stands with legs spread shoulder-width apart and hands behind her head. Always looking straight ahead, she slowly bends at the waist until her torso is parallel with the ground, and then slowly rises back up to the starting position (see Figures 24-4 and 24-5 in Session #24). Have her perform two sets of 12.

A FITNESS FRENZY

"I hated every minute of the training, but I said, don't quit. Suffer now and live the rest of your life as a champion."

—Muhammad Ali

Equipment Needed: 10 balls

Warm-Up Activities

- Footwork

Place eight cones or balls two to three feet apart. Have keepers perform three sets of each exercise. Stretch and rest as needed.

In and Out: The starting position is to the side of the cones. With a slight bend in the knees, while balancing on the balls of the feet, the goalkeeper should weave in and out of the cones, keeping her hips square, head up, eyes forward, and hands ready (see Figure 5-1 in Session #5).

Up and Over: The starting position is to the side of the cones. The leg nearest to the cone goes over first and then the second leg follows. With her knees coming up high, the goalkeeper should go up and over each cone, keeping her hips square, head up, eyes forward, and hands ready. Her feet should not touch or cross (see Figure 5-2 in Session #5).

Power Step: The starting position is directly facing the line of cones, one step to the side. The leg nearest the cone power-steps forward on a slight angle through the cones. The trail leg should follow—but never touch—the other leg. After each power step through the cones, the goalkeeper should freeze for a second in the set position, meaning she is ready to react to a shot. Throughout the exercise, she should stay on the balls of her feet for balance, with her head up eyes forward, knees slightly bent, and hands ready (see Figure 20-1 in Session #20).

Extended In and Out: Move every other cone one yard up so the cones make a zigzag pattern. The technique is the same as described in the In and Out exercise, except her first step should be big. The leg closest to the cone should be used to take the first step. Her first step should beat the cone. Be sure the goalkeeper keeps her balance when backpedaling (see Figure 7-2 in Session #7).

□ V-Sits

The goalkeeper sits on the ground with her legs out in front of her. The server delivers an underhand toss to one side. The goalkeeper dives at a forward angle toward the ball, trying to save the ball up toward her feet, thus creating a "V" when she saves the ball (see Figure 13-2 and 13-3 in Session #13). Have her perform two sets of 10 repetitions. *Coaching Notes: V-sits help goalkeepers warm up in two ways. First, they warm up her hands, shoulders, and neck, thus preparing her upper body for the task of diving. Second, they prepare her mentally to always attack the ball and dive toward the ball at a forward angle.*

□ Ball Gymnastics

Have keepers perform one set of eight repetitions of each exercise.

- The goalkeeper starts in a standing position, tosses the ball up in the air, performs a forward roll, and then catches the ball above her head at the highest point possible.
- The goalkeeper begins in a sitting position, tosses the ball up in the air, and then quickly stands up to catch the ball above her head at the highest point. For greater challenge, have the keeper try to stand up without using her hands.

Shot Stopping

Goalkeepers rotate every five shots and perform the following exercises. Have them perform two sets of five for each exercise. For the last three exercises, alternate the side of the goal.

- Goalkeeper stops shots from edge of the 18-yard box. Service is right at the goalkeeper.
- Same as in the previous exercise, except shots are played from an angle at a 12-yard distance and service is toward the near post.
- Goalkeeper begins exercise by falling to save a stationary ball on the ground at the far post, and then rises quickly to save a high ball tossed at the near post.
- Goalkeeper is in goal, and the non-working goalkeeper and server are at the top of the 18-yard box with a ball. The server dribbles in towards goal, while the goalkeeper advances and dives hands first to save the ball. After the save, she

returns to the goal line, and the non-working goalkeeper dribbles in from the other side. The server and non-working goalkeeper do not shoot the ball.

Strength/Fitness

Front Squat: Holding a ball in both hands with arms straight and away from her body, the goalkeeper performs a deep knee bend. Make sure her legs are shoulder width and she keeps her weight on her heels (see Figure 33-6 in Session #33). Have her perform two sets of 12 repetitions.

Forward Lunge: In a standing position, the goalkeeper lunges forward onto her right leg, and then pushes back to the standing position—using only her right leg (see Figures 33-7 and 33-8 in Session #33). Have her perform two sets of 10 repetitions.

Roll-Out Push-Ups: The goalkeeper starts out with her legs shoulder-width apart, upper body bent down, and her hands on a ball midway between her feet. She rolls forward on the ball until her body is in a push-up position. She performs a push-up, and then—without taking her hands off the ball or going down on her knees—she rolls back into the starting position (see Figure 2-6 in Session #2). Have her perform one set of eight.

Hungarian Sit-Ups: The goalkeepers sit close on the ground, facing opposite directions. Interlocking hands and keeping their legs straight and off the ground, they bring their legs up and around to the other side (see Figure 2-7 in Session #2). Have them perform two sets of 20.

13

Potluck

PICK YOUR FAVORITE

"The most important thing is to love your sport.
Never do it to please someone else. It has to be yours.
That is all that will justify the hard work needed to achieve success."

—Peggy Fleming, Olympic figure skater

Equipment Needed: A supply of balls and cones.

Key Coaching Points: Each goalkeeper picks her favorite warm-up activity, ball gymnastic, favorite exercise, and strength and fitness exercise. The following workout is my personal favorite.

Warm-Up Activity

□ Star

The goalkeeper begins in the center of the star, which is four-yards each direction from the center spot (see Figure 50-1). She listens for a command from the server to move "Up," "Back," "Right," or "Left." The goalkeeper always begins and ends in the center of the star. Have her perform each set at intervals of 30 seconds. Stretch as needed between sets.

- For the first set, the server only gives one command at a time.
- For the second set, the server gives two commands at a time.
- For the third set, the server gives three commands at a time.

□ V-Sits

The goalkeeper sits on the ground with her legs out in front of her. The server gives her an underhand toss to one side. The goalkeeper dives at a forward angle, trying to save the ball up toward her feet, creating a "V" when she saves the ball (see Figures

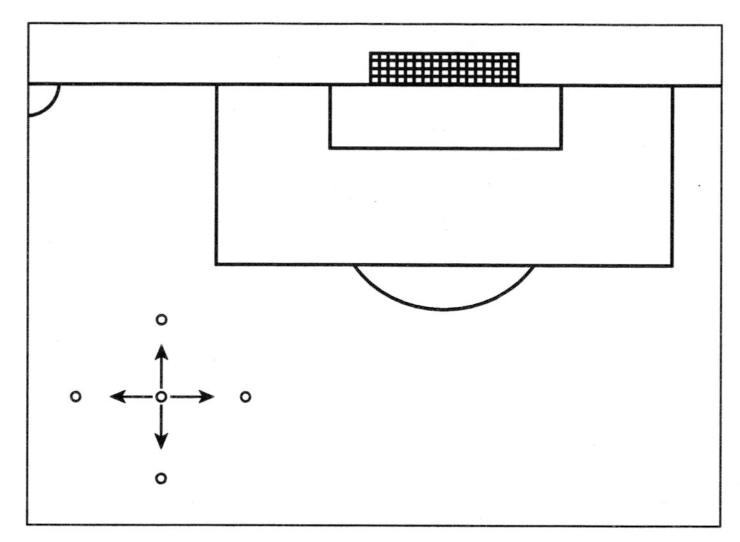

Figure 50-1

13-2 and 13-3 in Session #13). Have her perform two sets of 10 repetitions. *Coaching Notes: V-sits help goalkeepers warm up in two ways. First, they warm up her hands, shoulders, and neck, thus preparing her upper body for the task of diving. Second, they prepare her mentally to always attack the ball and dive toward the ball at a forward angle.*

□ Ball Gymnastics

Have the keepers perform one set of six repetitions of each exercise.

- The goalkeeper starts in a standing position, tosses the ball up in the air, performs a forward roll, and then catches the ball above her head at the highest point possible.
- The goalkeeper begins in a sitting position, tosses the ball up in the air, and then quickly stands up to catch the ball above her head at the highest point. For greater challenge, have her try to stand up without using her hands.

Near Post

The goalkeeper begins in the center of the goal on the goal line. On the server's command, she moves in a controlled manner up and around the cone, which is placed approximately four yards on an angle from the goal line and four yards from the near post. As soon as she is around the cone, she should set to receive a firm shot on the ground right inside the near post. The server should be approximately 10 yards away (see Figure 50-2). Have her perform two sets of eight on each side. *Coaching Note:*

Depending on the level and age of your goalkeeper, adjust the distance of the cone away from the goal line (the closer the cone is to the goal and the post, the easier the exercise).

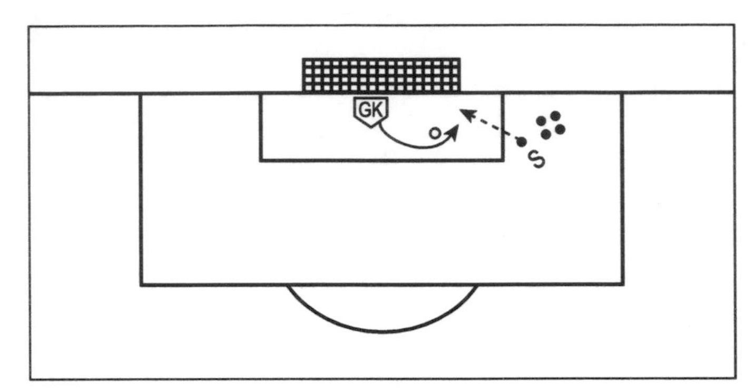

Figure 50-2

Rapid Fire

Line up 10 balls 12 to 14 yards from the goal line. The goalkeeper begins the exercise in her goalmouth at a comfortable distance from the balls. Without pausing, the server shoots the first five balls, and the non-working goalkeeper finishes the exercise by shooting the next five. The shots should be within one yard of the goalkeeper. Only pause long enough to give the goalkeeper a chance for each shot. Have them perform three sets of 10. *Coaching Note: For added fun, keep score and have the loser do push-ups.*

Strength/Fitness

Roll-Out Push-Ups: The goalkeeper starts out with her legs shoulder-width apart, upper body bent down, and her hands on a ball midway between her feet. She rolls forward on the ball until her body is in a push-up position. She performs a push-up, and then—without taking her hands off the ball or going down on her knees—she rolls back into the starting position (see Figure 2-6 in Session #2). Have her perform one set of 10.

Goalkeeper Sit-Ups: The goalkeepers lay on their backs with feet touching. Using one ball, they take turns throwing the ball back and forth, doing a sit-up every time they catch the ball (see Figure 3-6 in Session #3). Have them perform two sets of 25 reps.

Appendix A

Five-Minute Stretching Routine

Angie Taylor, MS, ATC
Assistant Athletic Trainer
Eastern Washington University

Stretching is the simplest of injury-prevention techniques. Goalkeeping places many physical demands on an athlete's body. A goalkeeper is required to quickly change the positioning of the body, as well as perform tasks repeatedly throughout a practice session or game. Increased flexibility can significantly reduce the risk of musculoskeletal injuries by reducing stress on the muscles and joints. Stretching following a workout is most beneficial in increasing flexibility because the muscle and joints are warm. This self-stretching routine targets the most common problem areas regarding flexibility. An immense number of stretches can be performed alone, or with a partner or apparatus. This five-minute routine is a thorough yet basic tool for flexibility training. Also, in regards to stretching, the longer or the more often the better.

Hamstring/Calf/Lateral Hip/Glute Series

Straight Leg Hamstring: Lie on back. Flex one hip while raising the leg. Place a towel around the heel and hold on to the ends of the towel. While keeping the knee straight, gently pull on the towel until a stretch is felt. Make sure to keep the hip on the ground, even if the leg does not go as far. Stretch should be felt in the lower hamstring, just above the knee. Hold for 10 to 15 seconds. Perform two times on each leg.

Bent Knee Hamstring: Lie on back. Bring one knee to chest and place one hand on the back of the thigh, pulling toward chest. Place the other hand on the back of the ankle and gently pull. Stretch should be felt in middle of the hamstring. Hold for 10 to 15 seconds. Perform two times on each leg.

Piriformis/Lateral Hip Stretch: Lie on back with both knees bent. Place the ankle of one leg on the thigh of the other leg. Grasp the lower leg with one hand and place the palm of other hand on inside of knee. Gently pull the lower leg toward the body and press the knee away. Stretch should be felt in outside of the hip and glute area. Hold for 10 to 15 seconds, and perform twice on each leg.

Lower-Back Stretch: Lie on back with arms out to the sides. Bend one knee and rotate the hips so that the knee crosses over the body. Stretch should be felt in the lower back. Hold for 10 to 15 seconds and perform twice on each side.

Seated Posterior Leg Stretch: Sit on the ground keeping the knees straight and the toes pulled up. Place a towel around the balls of the feet. Sitting with the back straight, gently pull the towel. If no stretch is felt, lean forward keeping the back straight. Stretch should be felt in the back of the legs. Hold for 10 to 15 seconds. Perform twice.

Hip Flexor Stretch: Kneel on one knee and place other foot in front so that the knee is bent to 90 degrees. Make sure that the hips stay square. Tighten the abdominal muscles and lean forward. Stretch should be felt in the front of the hip. Hold for 10 to 15 seconds and perform twice on each leg.

Groin/Adductor Stretch: Kneel on one knee and place the other foot halfway between front and side with the knee bent to 90 degrees. Tighten the abdominal muscles and lean toward the other leg. Stretch should be felt in the inner thigh. Adjust foot angle to optimize the stretch. Hold for 10 to 15 seconds and perform twice on each leg.

Appendix B

The Benefits of Strength Training

Darin Lovat, MS, CSCS, USAW Level 1 Club Coach
Head Strength and Conditioning Coach
Eastern Washington University

In this day and age, the majority of sport coaches have accepted that proper strength training can be of great benefit for their respective teams. While great improvements have been made in the modern training of athletes, some myths are still out there that prevent coaches and athletes from fully participating in proper training programs. In the 21st century, people still believe that lifting weights will make athletes "bulky" and "tight." Many of these types of beliefs stem from what modern culture has defined as weight training. Most people's knowledge of training stems from magazine publications such as *Muscle and Fitness and Men's Health*. While these magazines claim to be the leading sources of training information, most of them are nothing more than advertisements for nutrition supplements stuffed between pages of drug-induced bodybuilders. This current negative image is something that strength and conditioning professionals are trying to change. The information in the following pages should answer the "Why do I need to be doing this?" question that most athletes ask regarding their strength training programs.

Proper Weight Training

Olympic Lifts

Olympic-style weightlifting movements form the basis of the training philosophy at Eastern Washington University. The two Olympic lifts are the snatch and the clean and jerk, which both involve explosively lifting a barbell from the floor to overhead. While the two competitive lifts are rarely used in the training of athletes at Eastern, many variations of the Olympic weightlifting exercises are employed to do the following:

- Teach an athlete how to explode. Olympic weightlifters possess the ability to actively recruit as much muscle as possible in the shortest amount of time. This style of exercise forces an athlete to recruit the "fast twitch" muscle fibers in a rapid, coordinated fashion. A soccer athlete must do this exercise repeatedly during practices and games.

- Teach athletes to apply force from the center of the body to its extremities. This technique proves valuable to athletes who must impart force on another person or object. Some examples are beating an opposing player to the ball, making a diving save at the corner of the net, and winning headers.
- Force an athlete to accelerate heavy objects through varying degrees of resistance. Through different stages of the Olympic lifts, the body experiences differing degrees of perceived resistance as the weight is moved with maximum speed. These changes can be similar to those encountered out on the playing field.
- Teach an athlete to receive force from another moving object or body effectively. Upon learning this, athlete's bodies become conditioned to accept such forces. Examples include fighting off defenders, staying up during attempted slide tackles, and holding position during a corner kick.
- Effectively train the stretch-shortening cycle of muscle tissue. This cycle is employed in the muscles whenever an athlete has to apply force rapidly, such as in sprinting and jumping.
- Train movement patterns that are similar to the ones used in athletics. Soccer involves many short burst and quick stopping movements. The Olympic-style lifts teach athletes how to both explode and stop rapidly better than any other free-weight method.
- Many different Olympic, world-class athletes have been compared on a battery of tests including maximum jump height, speed over short distances, and flexibility. On these tests, Olympic weightlifters have had among the highest vertical jumps and have been second only to world-class sprinters and gymnasts in the short sprint and flexibility tests respectively. These results are even more impressive when one takes into consideration that these tests were hardly practiced by the weightlifting athletes. The fact that they performed so well can be attributed to their type of training. If these results are possible, then any athlete who is involved in sports that require speed and explosiveness should include Olympic-style weightlifting movements in their training programs.

Core and Lower-Body Strength

In all athletic events, the power an athlete exerts comes from the center of the body. It is then transferred to the extremities. Having a strong core (abdominals and lower back) is essential for sustaining desired performance over the course of a competitive season at the collegiate level. It becomes even more important at the professional level, where the season is even longer. Thinking of the body as a chain can help one understand the importance of core strength. The abdominals and lower back are the foundation of the body's chain. If these links are weak, then the rest of the body suffers. Too often, if an athlete's core is weak, then she may have problems other places, such as the knees and hips. When the core muscles are weak, they make other even more injury-prone parts of the body absorb and dissipate forces that place the athlete at risk for injury. Having a strong abdominal and lower-back region does two things:

- It increases a person's potential for increased power output over an extended period of time.
- It greatly reduces the chance of sustaining injuries to the lower back and lower extremities.

Leg strength is vital for top athletic performance day in and day out. However, along with the lower back and abdominals, the legs are often the most underdeveloped part of an athlete's body. The best way to increase lower-body strength is to include exercises that:

- Load the spine and hip.
- Make the athlete stand on his/her feet.
- Use multiple muscle groups (quadriceps, hamstrings, gluteus, lower back) in one movement.

The foundations for increasing lower-body strength for soccer athletes at Eastern Washington University are squatting and lunge movements. These movements are performed using one or two legs at the same time. They are also performed in every direction: forward, backward, and laterally. Squatting and lunging are two of the best lower-body strengthening exercises a soccer athlete can perform. Increased leg strength is the foundation for being able to sprint faster, stop quickly, and accelerate better. Being able to sprint, stop, and accelerate are all very desirable qualities for soccer athletes.

Two myths are common among soccer coaches regarding aggressive lower-body training that need to be explained:

- Working the legs makes players slower.
- Working the legs makes players less flexible

First of all, any resistance exercise that is executed with the correct resistance, within the correct repetition range, at the correct tempo, and within the correct range of motion will only *enhance* the development of fast twitch muscle fibers. When a greater number of fast twitch fibers are developed, guess what happens? That's right—soccer players become faster.

Secondly, any resistance exercise that is performed properly over a joint's full range of motion only *enhances* flexibility. Improved speed and flexibility as a result of proper lower-body training is well documented. Only ignorant and foolish coaches still believe in these myths.

Upper-Body Strength

Upper-body strength is of extreme importance for soccer athletes. Too often, the only method of measuring upper-body strength is the much-overrated bench press. While lying down flat and pressing the bar away from the body does greatly stimulate the large muscles of the upper body, it is simply no match for being able to put heavier weights overhead. Overhead strength is transferable to any sport. Pressing weights overhead not only works the entire shoulder region effectively, it also forces athletes to use their abdominal and lower-back muscles to help stabilize the body. As stated previously, abdominal and lower-back strength is critical to a soccer athlete's success in the long run.

Soccer has become a very physical game. With players being larger and faster, the collisions that occur are becoming more violent. Injuries to the shoulder joint are becoming much more common. Proper training of the shoulders and upper back can lessen the severity of and help prevent injuries to the shoulders.

Conclusion

Now that the information is available, no more excuses should be accepted as to why soccer athletes should not participate in a strength-training program. How many times do you see a great player miss an entire season or have her career cut short because of injuries? Answer: way too often. Obviously, not all injuries are preventable, and some are just plain old bad luck, but the stronger and better-conditioned athletes will play better and have longer careers than the weaker ones. If all soccer athletes aggressively adhere to a well-designed strength and power program, they will see the benefits of it on the playing field for a long time.

About the Author

Tamara Browder Hageage is the goalkeeper coach and assistant women's soccer coach at Eastern Washington University. She began her soccer career at the age of six. At Woodward High School in Toledo, she was a four-year starter in goal for the boys' varsity team. She was a member of the Ohio-North State Team from 1990 until 1997. She was selected to the regional team/pool from 1992 to 1997, and was invited to the national team tryouts in 1992 and 1993.

Tamara's college career began in 1990 as a scholarship athlete at Colorado College, where her team made it to the NCAA Division I Final Four. She completed her last three years of collegiate eligibility at the University of Washington, where she received MVP honors in 1991 and still holds several records, including most goalkeeper saves in a season (106 in 1991), most goalkeeper shutouts in a season (8 in 1991), and most goalkeeper saves in a match (14 vs. Michigan State, 9/23/92).

After graduating from Washington in 1994, Tamara returned to Toledo to complete a master's degree and began her coaching career by helping to lead St. Ursula High School to the regional finals. She also played on a men's semi-professional team.

In 1995, Tamara played with the Cincinnati Leopards of the Women's United States Interregional Soccer League (U.S.I.S.L) and helped the team reach the final six. In 1996 and 1997, she continued to play in the U.S.I.S.L as a captain for the Cleveland Eclipse. During this time, Tamara also worked as the assistant coach for the University of Toledo.

In 1998, Tamara headed to Russia to play for Ryazan F.C. in the Russian First Division. Next, she played for Denmark's F.C. Fortuna, one of the biggest, most successful women's professional clubs in Europe. She was the first American to sign a professional contract in the Danish First Division and the first to win the club's most valuable player award. Tamara also played professionally for Laval in Montreal, Quebec.

After retiring from professional soccer in 1999 due to congenital foot problems, Tamara was named the head women's soccer coach at Northview High School in Sylvania, Ohio. She led Northview to their highest ranking ever in the state and was named the 1999 District Coach of the Year. In July 2000, Tamara took over the women's soccer program at Eastern Washington University with her husband, George Hageage.

In 2004, Tamara earned her advanced national diploma from the National Soccer Coaches Association of America and helped lead the Eastern Eagles to a piece of the Big Sky Conference title. In the summer of 2005, Tamara was one of two athletic directors for the People to People Sports Ambassador Program and led a group of 600 players and 34 coaches in a tournament in Haarlem, Holland.

Tamara and her husband, George, have a son, George IV, who was born in January 2004. She is also the author of *Effective Soccer Goalkeeping for Women*, and is the featured speaker on two videos, *Effective Soccer Goalkeeping for Women, Volumes 1 and 2*. In addition to coaching responsibilities at EWU, Tamara focuses her professional energy on helping coaches and goalkeepers become more effective by serving as the director of coaching for the Spokane Valley Junior Soccer Association, working with the Washington State Olympic Development goalkeeping staff, and volunteering as a coach for Spokane's TOPSoccer program.